W9-BSH-655

Long Way Round

THE ILLUSTRATED EDITION

Long Way Round
THE ILLUSTRATED EDITION

CHASING SHADOWS ACROSS THE WORLD

Ewan McGregor *and* Charley Boorman

WITH ROBERT UHLIG
ABRIDGED BY KATI NICHOLL

TIME WARNER
BOOKS

For my love Olivia for putting up with it all and my children
Doone and Kinvara, my little angels.

Charley Boorman

I dedicate this book to the many friendly people Charley and
I came across on our journey and who helped us on our way.
Without you we'd still be out there.

Ewan McGregor

Time Warner Books
First published in Great Britain in October 2005 by Time Warner Books
Reprinted 2005
Copyright © Long Way Round Limited, 2005
Map copyright © John Gilkes, 2005
The moral right of the author has been asserted.

All rights reserved.
No part of this publication may be reproduced, stored in a retrieval system,
or transmitted, in any form or by any means, without the prior permission
in writing of the publisher, nor be otherwise circulated in any form of binding
or cover other than that in which it is published and without a similar
condition including this condition being imposed on the subsequent purchaser.

A CIP catalogue record for this book
is available from the British Library.

ISBN 13: 978–0–316–73170–6
ISBN 10: 0–316–73170–6

Printed and bound in Great Britain
by Butler & Tanner

Time Warner Books
An imprint of
Time Warner Book Group UK
Brettenham House
Lancaster Place
London WC2E 7EN

www.twbg.co.uk

Contents

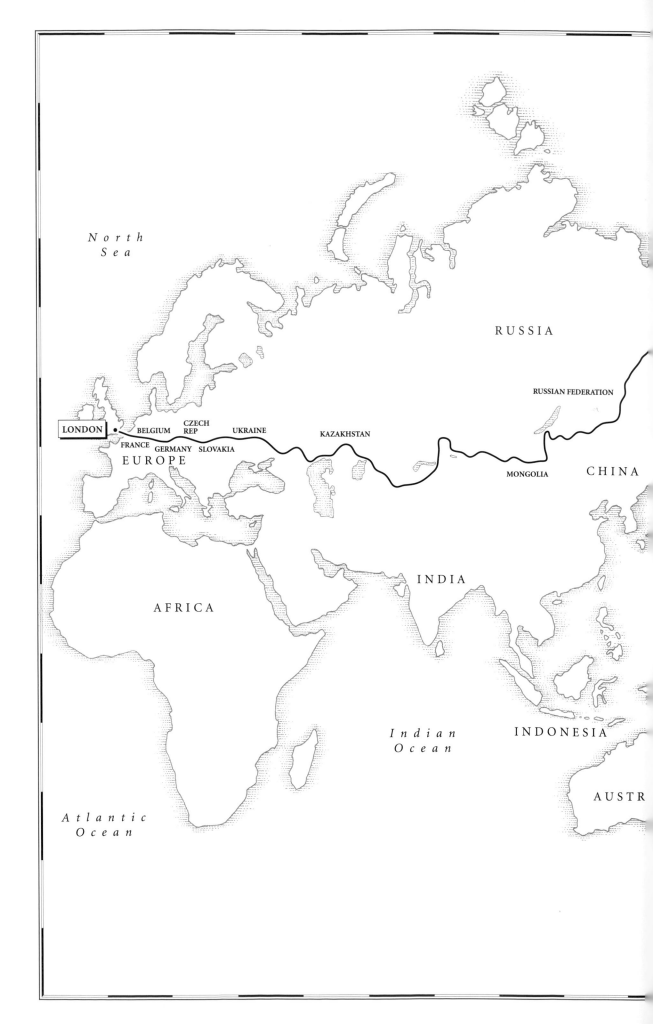

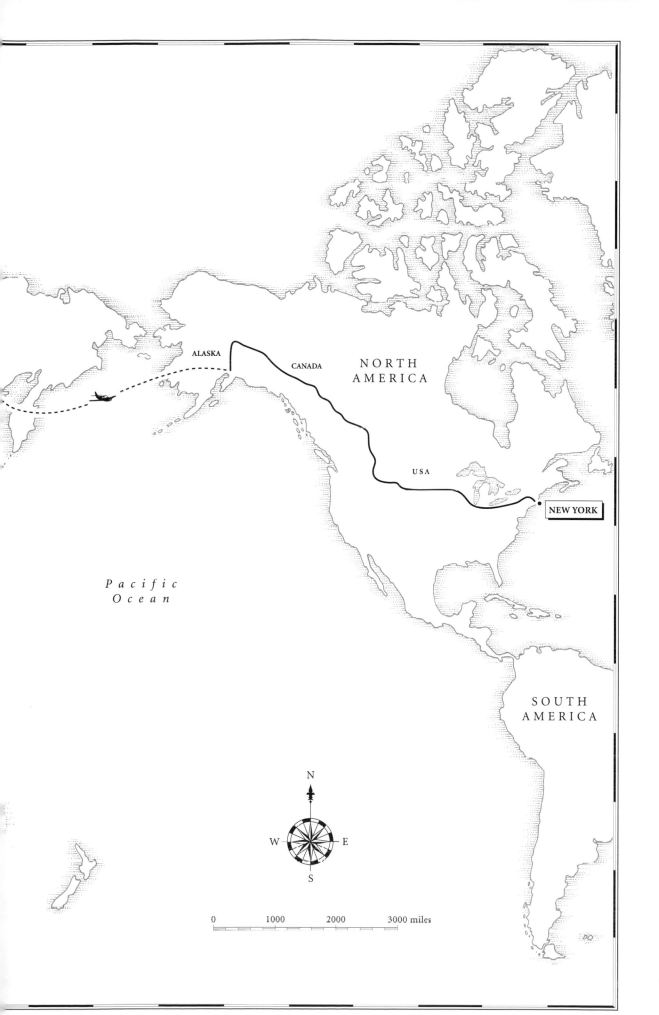

ALASKA

CANADA

NORTH
AMERICA

USA

NEW YORK

*Pacific
Ocean*

SOUTH
AMERICA

N

W   E

S

0   1000   2000   3000 miles

1 ▶ ▶ ▶

▶ ▶ ▶ ▶

On yer bike

EWAN: Every journey begins with a single step. In our case it was eight years ago, when Charley walked up to me in Casey's, a pub at Sixmilebridge in County Clare. Except for an eager smile, there was nothing in the way of an introduction.

'You ride bikes,' he said.

'Yeah,' I replied, taken aback by the gregarious stranger.

With our wives and daughters we had moved into cottages on location in Ireland to shoot *Serpent's Kiss*, and it was the kick-off party on the eve of the first day's shooting. Charley and I had a lot in common. We were married with daughters only a few months old, we'd been successful actors for some time and we were facing weeks of working closely together. There was a lot we could have talked about, but Charley has an instinct for cutting straight to the subject closest to a person's heart.

'Yeah . . . yeah, I ride a '78 Motoguzzi,' I said, referring to my first big bike, a heavy Italian machine built like a tractor. And with that, the evening dissolved into a long night of biker anecdotes.

The more we got to know each other, the more we found we had in common, and we got on so well that by the time of the wrap party I had asked Charley to be godfather to my daughter, Clara.

Events soon turned our relationship into something even deeper.

I had flown to Chicago and Los Angeles to make an episode of *ER*, coincidentally called *Long Way Round*. While I was on set, lying in a hospital bed with tubes up my nose, by some horrible irony my Clara was being rushed into hospital in London with a severe case of meningitis.

I flew straight home to spend the next fortnight sitting at my wee girl's bedside with my wife, Eve. It was a terrible time and I turned to Charley, who had himself gone through a difficult period when his eldest daughter, Doone, had been severely ill.

One afternoon after Charley had visited us at the Chelsea and Westminster Hospital I saw him out. It was so serious, what was happening to Clara upstairs, and he turned to me and simply said:

'It's okay. It can get better.'

He gave me a big hug, then swung his leg over his Honda XR600R, pulled out into the traffic, lifted the front wheel and hoicked a huge wheelie all the way down the Fulham Road. That wheelie was so brilliantly inappropriate that it cut through my anxiety, lifting my spirits more than any words could have done. Just when I needed it, he really cheered me up and in that moment our friendship was sealed.

CHARLEY: When I met Ewan, I immediately recognised a kindred spirit. Someone with big passions in his life, and with biking at the centre of them. I've been obsessed with bikes for as long as I can remember. When I was about six years old my father, John Boorman, was filming *Zardoz* in Ireland with Sean Connery. One weekend, Sean's son Jason came to visit. Jason was quite a bit older than me and spent most of his stay forcing me to push him up and down on a little monkey bike. Eventually he let me have a go. I promptly fell off, but that one moment, that twist of the grip, the roar of the engine, the smell of the exhaust and the thrill of the speed was enough. I was hooked.

Later I persuaded my parents to let me buy a Yamaha 100 miniature trials bike that I've kept to this day and by the time I was twelve, I had a 125cc and I was into motocross whenever I wasn't making films. I passed my test when I was about twenty-one and living in London. Then I got my Kawasaki Zephyr 750, my first big bike.

EWAN: My biking baptism can be summed up in two words: teenage love. My first girlfriend was petite with short mousy blonde hair, and I was mad about her.

I was a day pupil, she was a boarder at Morrison's Academy in Crieff, a small Perthshire town. She and I went out for a while when I was about thirteen or fourteen. She was very sweet-natured and her right breast was the first girl's breast that I ever touched. In a bush off Drummond Terrace.

Our romance came to an abrupt end when she started going out with another guy. He rode a 50cc road bike first and then a 125. And whereas I had always walked my girlfriend back to Ogilvy House, where she boarded, and snogged her at the gate, suddenly she was going back with this guy. He would meet her at the back gate, snog her and then he would go screeching around Ogilvy House on his motorbike.

I was nearly sixteen by then and heartbroken. Then one day my mum and I passed Buchan's, the local bike shop. There was a light blue 50cc bike on display right at the front of the shop. I didn't know what make it was, or if it was any good. All I knew was that I could get it in three or four months' time. I could ride it at sixteen and maybe get my girlfriend back.

I'd ridden my first bike when I was about six. My father, Jim, was chairman of the Crieff Round Table and had organised an event for disadvantaged children. It was a kind of *Jim'll Fix It* and one small boy's fix-it was to ride a motorbike. My father organised a wee red Honda 50cc and after the kid had a go, they asked me if I wanted a ride. I clambered on and shot off. I thought it was just the best thing. I loved the smell of it, the sound of it, the look of it, the high-pitched screaming of the engine. So when I looked through Buchan's window in Perth that day, I knew somehow I had to have that bike.

Driven to desperation by my desire, I made a series of promises to my mum: I won't leave town. I'll be very safe. I won't take any risks. I won't do anything stupid. But, in truth, I was making it up as I was going along.

'I'll only go thirty miles an hour, just please let me have the bike,' I begged.

'I'll speak to your dad,' Mum replied. But my parents never gave in. 'If something happened to you, I couldn't possibly forgive myself,' my mother told me.

She was probably right, too. At the time that I was begging for a bike I'd already had a close scrape with a 100cc four-stroke belonging to George Carson, the school laboratory technician. I was playing Sganarelle in a school production of the Molière play. During a break in rehearsals I casually popped the question to Mr Carson.

'Can I have a go on your motorbike, sir?'

'Yeah, of course,' he replied, not knowing I didn't have a clue how to ride it.

The bike was in an alleyway up the side of the refectory building. I managed to kick-start it, but, unable to control the clutch, stalled it three times. On the fourth attempt, I took off, zooming down the alleyway until I crashed smack into a wall, bending the wheel and snapping the handlebars.

The bill for the damage came to more than £80, a fortune in those days and one that took me months of working as a dishwasher and waiter at the Murray Park Hotel to pay back.

So when my mother refused my pleas for a bike part of me understood her concerns but the rest of me knew there was something missing. Spiritually I was already a biker but I just didn't have a bike.

A year or so later I left home for drama school. First to Fife for a year and then down to the Guildhall in London – and as soon as I graduated and started working, I headed for a bike shop in Kentish Town in north London. Sitting in that shop was a Honda 100cc bike that I could ride on a car licence. I bought it straightaway and loved it. For the first time, I felt totally independent. And I wore all the gear.

One day I was sitting in traffic dressed like the archetypal greasy biker: denim jacket, leather jacket, an open-faced helmet with goggles. I really looked the part. And approaching me, on the other side of the column of traffic, was a very cool rider, dressed almost the same. As he drew level, Zen biker nodded over to me, across the top of a car bonnet, to say 'How you doing?' I nodded back. The lights turned green and we moved away. As the traffic cleared, Zen biker could see that, while he was sitting on a big Harley-Davidson, I was straddling a wee Honda 100cc. His withering look could have shrivelled a pomegranate.

That embarrassing episode only strengthened my resolve to get my biker's licence and

to buy a large bike. The day I passed my test, I bought a very old 1970s Motoguzzi Le Mans. I loved the look of it, but it was like riding a tractor. It was a dog. But it was perfect for me – noisy, oily, good-looking and messy. My only regret about the Guzzi, which I restored and customised until it was a beauty, is that I eventually sold it.

Then, while filming an episode of *Kavanagh QC*, I met a beautiful French production designer. I fell head over heels in love with Eve Mavrakis and we married soon afterwards.

From the early days of our romance, Eve made it clear that she didn't care for bikes at all. She thought they were dangerous. And if Eve seriously asked me to stop riding, I would hang up my leathers, but she knows that bikes are my passion and, because of that, my wife has always tolerated my bike riding.

It wasn't until Sasha Gustav, a Russian photographer friend, lent me his sports bike that I found out for myself how much fun they are.

It was the first brand new bike I had ridden and going down Haverstock Hill in Hampstead I pulled away gently from the lights and looked down at the speedometer to discover I was already doing 80mph. Alarmed, I hit the brakes and stopped almost instantaneously. I was gobsmacked. I decided there and then to get a new bike and to make it a sports bike, a brand new Ducati 748.

Importing the Ducati from Europe made it slightly cheaper but I had to pay cash. Every few weeks I would bowl into the *Star Wars* accounts department – I was filming *The Phantom Menace* – to ask for an advance against my wages and it all had to be authorised.

One afternoon I got a phone call from Rick McCallum, the producer and George Lucas's right-hand man. He wanted to speak to me about the bike. My first thought was: 'Oh fuck, I'm in trouble.'

'George and I want to know how much this bike is costing you?' Rick asked. I told him, thinking I was about to be castigated for bothering the production accountants.

'George and I would like to buy it for you,' Rick said. I was stunned. For the next few years, I rode around on what was in effect George Lucas's bike, until I passed it on to Charley, who rides it to this day.

My contract usually forbids me from riding a bike while shooting a movie. The only location where I was allowed to ride to work was Australia; I spent almost two years there on and off, shooting *Moulin Rouge* and the second and third *Star Wars* episodes and when I first met Baz Luhrman, the director of *Moulin Rouge*, I told him that if he wanted me to sign up for eight months to rehearse and shoot his film I had to be allowed to ride a bike.

'I act. I am with my wife and kids. And I ride motorbikes. That's it, that's all I do,' I said. 'I cannot stay off bikes for eight months.'

When I leave work on a motorbike, pull on my helmet and move off, it doesn't matter if I've had a good day or not. By the time I get home my mind has been cleared of any troubles. And motorcycling gives me anonymity and I don't have much of that in my life. When I'm flashing around on my bike with my helmet on I'm just another geezer on the road and that's nice. But, above all, there's something about riding a bike the concentration and the single-mindedness of it, and the desire to get it right, taking a corner fast without losing control, doing it beautifully, getting into a groove and winning the battle between your head telling you to do one thing, the bike wanting to do another and your body in between – that I miss like hell if I don't get to ride it every day.

CHARLEY: For most bikers, commuting around town is never enough. The urge to go faster and further takes over, and the open road beckons. But my obsession with bikes and speed was accompanied by increasingly close scrapes with injuries and a series of almost fatal accidents. Racing along twisty country roads with a mate, I entered a corner far too fast and I knew there was no way I was going to come out of that hairpin in one piece. Looking around for an exit route, I spotted a clear run-off directly ahead. Then I noticed a tiny little lip at the edge of the tarmac. At a safe speed, I would have passed over it without incident, but at more than 100mph it was going to cause serious trouble.

Moments later, my front tyre hit the lip, denting the rim. Then the back wheel went over it and the rear swing arm snapped. The bike went down and completely disintegrated, leaving me lying in the long grass with the remnants of the bike still beneath me.

'Charley, Charley, where are you?' It was David Healey, one of the many riders I used to meet for Sunday morning burn-ups to the coast. Dazed, I popped up from the grass like a startled meerkat. Bits of bike were scattered in a wide circle around me. My back and one of my shoulders hurt like hell, but it was the bike, not me, that was written off.

'Charley,' David said. 'You need a track day. You can do all this, much faster, but in an environment where there's less chance of you killing yourself.'

My first day at Snetterton, a simple, fast two-mile racetrack, was a revelation. It was the only time in my life that I ended a day thinking that if I had known about this when I was younger I would have made a career of it. It was also a terrible moment. I realised then what I really wanted to do with my life, but I was too old to do it.

EWAN: I soon followed Charley on to the racetrack. I'd had fewer close calls than he had, although exaggerated accounts of my falling off a Honda Blackbird had made the newspapers, which reported that I had narrowly escaped a fatal 180mph collision on a tour of the Scottish Highlands with my father in March 1999 when I should have been at the Oscar's ceremony in Hollywood. In fact, my rear wheel had slipped sideways on a diesel spill, tipping me off the bike at about 30mph more than a week after the Academy Awards.

My first track day was an event organised by Ducati at the Brands Hatch Indy circuit. Carl Fogarty, the legendary four-time World Superbike champion, was to be there and Ducati had asked me to join them. Arriving at Brands Hatch, I found the flies had broken on my particularly garish two-piece leather suit, given to me by *Bike* magazine when I'd done a photo shoot on my Motoguzzi for them. Asked what colour I wanted I said: 'Well, my bike's yellow. So maybe something yellow and black.' I was actually thinking of something predominantly black with a little bit of yellow piping. When the suit arrived it was like a diagonal chequered flag, all yellow and black squares, like a rotten banana. The boots were pink, purple and green – absolutely awful. And here I was, turning up for a track day – my first ever – with a bunch of bike journalists, and my flies were gaping wide open. Someone gave me some silver gaffer tape and I taped it over the crotch of my fluorescent-nightmare leather suit. It wasn't the greatest look.

Ducati paired me off with the oldest participant. As we walked down to the track, he asked me how fast I was. 'Oh, pretty quick,' I replied. The old guy told me he was worried about the pace. 'We'll just take it steady at first,' he suggested. We eased out on to the track, I tucked in behind him, and then he and all the other biking journalists just evaporated into thin air. Taking it easy, apparently. I hadn't been riding bikes for long enough to know the essentials: what gear to be in, how to keep the racing line and how to make a bike really move. But the learning curve is very steep on a track day and it didn't take long to learn the ropes. Hanging off your bike, your backside nearly scraping the tarmac, is a very strange thing to do, but it's the most exhilarating experience I've ever had. Even now, after many track days, my nerves will be shredded before the first session because racing is all about telling your brain to ignore its natural instincts, particularly on corners. Resisting until the very last moment, braking as late as you can, the whole back end of the bike lifting, trying to overtake itself as you struggle to do everything as smoothly and gently as possible, while your brain screams at you to slow down. It's a fabulous feeling when you get it right.

However, riding a bike is also about taking your time, cruising the highways, letting the road take you wherever it's going and not worrying about the destination, just enjoying the journey. A few years ago, I rode from London to my parents-in-law's home in north-east France. I didn't want to be recognised so I shaved my head into a Mohawk. After a day riding through central France, I stopped at a campsite at the Tarn Gorge and put my tent up. Dressed in shorts and a vest, with my six-inch Mohican and a large, freshly tattooed heart incorporating my wife and daughters' names on one bared shoulder, I entered the local bar. Sipping a drink, I was just about to ask the barman if I could book a table that evening when a customer looked at me as if I was a piece of dirt, with real hatred in his eyes. This Frenchman clearly thought I was despicable, worthy only of his contempt because of my appearance. It shocked me.

I crossed the road to a restaurant with dozens of empty tables inside and outside and asked for a table for later that evening. The waitress looked at the barman. They both looked at me, and then she said simply: '*Non.*'

I couldn't believe it. 'It's just for me – *pour moi.*'

'*Non.*'

'How about out of sight?'

'*Non.*'

I crawled back into my tent and went to sleep hungry and thirsty, surrounded by hundreds of happy British holidaymakers. Because of their presence on campsites across France, I'd shaved my hair into a Mohican to avoid detection. My disguise had succeeded so comprehensively that now I couldn't even buy a meal in a local bar.

But short breaks like this made me hanker for more, and gradually a trip started to take shape in my head. One Saturday afternoon I bought a very basic world map, spread it out and indulged in a bit of daydreaming. My wife had grown up in China, so I thought of riding there. Then I noticed that if I headed from Mongolia north into Siberia, instead of south to China, it wasn't that much further east to the edge of Asia.

Once there, it was only a relatively short leap across the Bering Strait to Alaska, and from Alaska, I reckoned, it would be hardtop all the way across North America. London to New York – the long way round: it had an appealing, exciting ring to it. I was looking at it when Charley phoned. 'I think you ought to come over for dinner,' I said.

By the time Charley and Olly arrived, I had made up my mind. Charley needed little persuading. My wife thought it might be just another madly ambitious scheme and, because it seemed so far away, immediately said: 'Of course you should go.' I had three more films to shoot – *Big Fish*, the third episode of *Star Wars* and *Stay* – then I would be free. I'd take three or four months off and we'd do the trip in the spring of 2004.

The first thing we did was to buy *The Adventure Motorcycling Handbook*. The first word of chapter one leapt from the page. 'Prepare,' it warned. 'As a rule a first time,

...the Long Way Round team

Cameraman and third rider Claudio von Planta.

Our fantastic production team (left to right): Jo Melling, Lucy Adams, Charley Boorman, Asia Mackay, Lucy Trujillo, Ewan McGregor and Rachel Newnham.

With our partners, Russ Malkin and, far right, David Alexanian.

Team doctor Vasiliy Nischenko and Russian fixer Sergey Grabovets.

Second cameraman James Simak.

multinational, trans-continental journey such as crossing Africa, the Americas or Asia needs at the very least one year of preparation. If you're heading right around the world, double that time.'

Two years! It was out of the question for both of us, yet the book said it would take that long to plan the journey and map out the route, organise visas, permits and other documentation, select and prepare the right motorbike, learn basic medical and mechanics' skills, get the vaccinations, source the camping equipment and motorcycle spares, learn languages, get fit and generally prepare ourselves.

Then we hit on a way of making it work: we would film the trip and sell it as a television series. Surely there would be interest in two well-known actors circumnavigating the globe and that would finance a production company to help us with the preparation. We would concentrate on the bikes, the physical preparation and choosing the equipment. The production staff would help us with the paperwork, source the equipment and deal with logistics. If we produced it ourselves, we would retain control of the filming and ensure the spirit of the trip – two friends alone on the road, surviving on their wits, a friendship united in adversity – would not be forgotten. Charley would find the producers.

CHARLEY: Fortunately I had the business card of a very ambitious and energetic producer I'd met at a party. Russ Malkin was brash and cocky – essential qualities in a good producer – and ran a production company, called Image Wizard. And he was a biker, so he understood the passion for speed and the draw of the open road. Russ seemed to be just the man we needed.

Fortunately Ewan hit it off with Russ and we went on a tour of big league independent television production companies. At every single one we heard the same spiel: 'Yeah, yeah, we can do that. Not a problem. We'll get the BBC involved. They'll put up the money. Leave it to us. We'll take care of it all.' All very impressive, but our dream of two mates on the road was in danger of being taken over by corporate executives with ponytails and baseball caps. If we were going to make a television series, then we wanted to dictate the terms. But how?

Russ's answer was to enlist David Alexanian, an old friend from Los Angeles, who made low-budget independent feature films. With his sister Alexis, David specialised in projects that other producers shied away from. Russ said he needed David to broker an American deal. We met David and immediately liked him. He was clearly a player, a typical LA dealmaker. Most importantly, David was also a biker.

In September Russ, David and I flew to Sydney, where Ewan was finishing shooting on *Revenge of the Sith*, episode three of the *Star Wars* prequels. We hired two Yamaha Super

Ténéré trail bikes and took off into the outback, where David and Russ shot a video of us that we could use to pitch our idea to broadcasters.

After *Star Wars*, Ewan flew to New York to shoot *Stay*. He'd taken only eight days off in the previous twelve months and had lined the inside of his trailer on the *Stay* set in New York with maps of the countries we hoped to pass through and was meticulously planning the journey. In London, however, nothing was going right. We had no bikes or offices, no money, no staff, no camping equipment, no bike gear. Nothing but a dream and Ewan badgering us to get a television deal double-quick.

EWAN: In December, Russ and David flew to the US to meet with my Los Angeles agents who weren't sure that people would be interested in our television series and without TV support we would really struggle to finance the trip.

Our dream trip was in jeopardy – and my immediate response was that we would have to find some way to fund the trip ourselves. I was about to broach the subject with my wife when she said: 'You should start looking into a way of doing the trip without David and Russ, without any television deal or any other way of funding it. Without anything. Just look into how you are going to do the trip, funding it yourself.'

Eve's support restored our confidence. So we phoned David and Russ and told them to stay in L.A. But they had already met with William Morris, another large TV and film agency, who seemed excited and had lined up a series of meetings with broadcasters in January.

Meanwhile, in London we were searching for offices. We needed somewhere like a garage to prepare our bikes, but with office space for the production staff and an editing suite. For weeks we trudged around premises all over the city. Depressed by the troubles we'd had and bored by visiting empty, unsuitable buildings, Charley rolled up outside an unprepossessing block in Shepherd's Bush in west London a few days before Christmas. He was on the point of not bothering to view the property, but when he went inside it was a revelation. It had a workshop which opened straight on to the street with a roll-up metal shutter to let the bikes in. There was a kitchen and office downstairs and more rooms upstairs. It was perfect. With only days left to Christmas, our adventure was suddenly taking shape. All we needed now was to test and get hold of some bikes, kit them out with touring equipment, order spares, source some camping gear, work out the route, organise visas and documentation, do some off-road training, and secure a television deal to pay for it all. So not much pressure then.

▶ ▶ ▶

From chaos to bliss

DEPARTURE DAY

zero

EWAN: From the moment we decided to ride around the world, Charley was convinced we should ride customised dirt bikes built by KTM, a small Austrian company. 'I've always wanted the KTM,' he said. 'It answers all the requirements I would need for this trip. Plus it has that GF, that grin factor, about it. It's more fun to ride. And I think that the KTM guys are much more fun and up for a bit of a laugh.'

But I needed more convincing, so early January found us outside the Abercrave Inn, near BMW's off-road training facility in the Brecon Beacons in south Wales. It was a miserable day as a squad of BMW engineers and executives led us through the 1150 GS Adventure, their top-of-the-range endurance touring-bike. Shaft-driven and stacked with servo-booster ABS brakes, a huge 1150cc Boxer engine, heated grips, a 30 litre tank for a 200-mile range, and loads of gadgets, it was a massive, heavy machine.

At BMW's off-road facility in the Brecon Beacons.

Charley and I sped off for a couple of hours, first on local roads then off-road on BMW's 2100-acre test area. After the ride, even Charley had to concede he was surprised by the BMW. 'They were a lot better than I thought they were going to be,' he said. 'But it's still fucking heavy.'

I thought the BMW was a beautiful machine. Two days later we were at KTM's offices on a nondescript industrial estate in Milton Keynes. From the moment we entered the building, Charley's face bore a grin that reached from ear to ear. 'Ooh, look at that,' he exclaimed. Right in front of us stood two gleaming bikes, a 640cc and the 950 Adventurer. As far as Charley was concerned, BMW didn't stand a chance.

We tested the 640 and 950 on KTM's test ground, a scrappy area of concrete beside a disused airfield. The KTMs performed brilliantly. The choice was between the KTM 640, which was lighter and better suited to off-road biking, and the KTM 950 Adventurer, which would be hard work off-road but which would cruise happily at 90 or 100mph on the thousands of miles of hardtop across North America. Our hearts were set on the bigger machine.

By lunchtime, Charley was so enthused he didn't want to leave the test track. 'It's just fantastic, it's everything that I thought it would be,' he said. Then Russ asked which bike we would choose if we had to set off immediately on a long journey.

'When you ask that,' I said, 'and there's the KTM sitting next to the BMW GS Adventure and I have to ride to Scotland right now, my immediate thought is that I'd go on the GS.'

Charley immediately cut in: 'But it's so . . . so . . . there's no excitement in it. BMW, you know . . . it's like their cars. I mean, they're lovely cars but they're boring to drive. You sit there and everything's functional.'

'The BMW is practical,' I said, 'because they absolutely fucking do what they're meant to do. Which is keep going for a very long time. And a lot of the KTM guys we just met were slightly nervous about taking the bike around the world. Whereas the fucking BMW has been round the world for the last fifty years.'

David cut in: 'You know what it looks like? The KTM sits there in the drive and it looks like a supermodel. It's, like, do you want to go out with Claudia Schiffer tonight? I mean, it's the sexiest fucking bike on the planet.'

We couldn't be happier: learning how to fix our bikes.

'Or do you want to go out with the BMW,' Charley added, 'which is one of the kitchen girls from the cooking programme.'

'Absolutely. You know you're going to get laid,' David added, 'so it's . . .'

'Two fat ladies or two supermodels,' Charley chipped in.

'Listen, this is a fucking nice problem to have,' I said. 'This is a high-class dilemma. Okay? Which fantastic motorcycle will we choose? So let's not lose sight of that.'

The next week we visited Honda. After a test ride, at last we agreed on something: Honda was too corporate and its bike was not what we were looking for.

By the end of January, Charley had got his way. The grin factor won, and by the time we went to meet Erlan Idrissov, the Kazakh ambassador, at his embassy in London, even I was enthusing about the Austrian bike. All we had to do now was persuade KTM to back us. Knowing they didn't have the resources of a company such as BMW, we had downgraded our expectations of sponsorship. All we wanted was a small financial contribution to the cost of the trip and four 950 Adventurers plus necessary spare parts.

KTM told us they would bring Thomas Junkers, a German film-maker who had ridden the 950 Adventurer to Siberia, to a meeting at which we hoped to finalise the deal. Charley said we had to be careful. 'KTM are bringing this guy who's done it, and they want him to have a look at our schedule. But he could just poo-poo it.'

The next day Georg Opitz, KTM's marketing representative, arrived in London with Junkers, a huge, fleshy beast who had very few words of encouragement. Large tracts of north-west Kazakhstan were to be avoided, he said, because the Soviets used it as a biological weapons test ground. 'There is a lot of throat disease around here because of whatever the Soviets were doing,' he said loftily.

North-east Kazakhstan was also to be avoided: 'No, no, no. These roads are not good,' Junkers insisted. 'Until 1989, this was the area for the nuclear bombs' . . . 'This is the only way you can go, whatever they tell you' . . . 'You can go there, but it is an area totally destroyed and with a high radiation. Very high.'

We had arranged with the Kazakh ambassador in London – who had assured us his young country was safe, beautiful and well worth visiting – to pass into Russia through a border usually restricted to freight traffic.

'You are sure? This area is normally a no-go area,' Thomas said categorically. 'Here you will find military. It is a major problem.'

And so it went on. The borders we wanted to use would be closed, according to Thomas. The routes we wanted to take would be impassable, he said. The permits, visas and border documents that our back-up team were organising would be worthless in the face of local bureaucracy. The contacts we had made with ambassadors, local police and the governments of Kazakhstan, Mongolia and Russia would not help us at all. And as for our maps, they were useless.

His harshest criticisms were targeted at our plans for eastern Siberia, where we knew we would face our toughest test on the Road of Bones from Yakutsk to Magadan on the Pacific coast. 'You want to take fourteen days for this?'

'I think so,' Charley said.

'What do you think if I tell you now you need six weeks for this one?' Thomas barked.

Again and again, Thomas shook his head and tutted. We knew we had lost the battle to convince the man with KTM's ear. Our only hope was that KTM had the balls to back us.

Two days later, on Friday 13th, the call came. Russ walked into the workshop after speaking on the phone to Georg. 'Bad news,' he said. 'We love the project, Georg said, but Thomas Junkers said there were bits about Siberia that he was worried . . .'

KTM, for all its hard-core image, was concerned that its bikes were not up to carrying two actors on a holiday trip around the world.

The news hit Charley like a ton of bricks. 'I feel like my whole world has just been . . . just been taken from under me,' he wailed.

I said: 'You know we now have to look at whether we go on the BMWs. What do we do? We have to look at our options now.'

Charley's response was immediate: 'We'll do it with BMW and show them what a fucking great big mistake they made!'

CHARLEY: KTM saying no was a bombshell. I was really impressed that Russ went immediately to BMW and that they came back straight away. They offered us so much, expressing great happiness and joy and pride at being part of the project. There were no questions about whether we could or couldn't do it. They felt it was exactly what their bike had been made for. We said, what about eastern Siberia? They said, part of the adventure is to try. I was really happy now to go on a BMW.

Most of all, I was really impressed with Ewan. He had wanted to go on a BMW right from the off, but he was going with the KTM for me and I really loved him for it.

EWAN: On Wednesday 14 April, shortly after 9 a.m., we set off. Ahead of us, three continents stretched eastwards. With 20,000 miles, 108 days and 19 time zones to go, we roared away from our friends, family and the team cheering behind us. Turning the corner, we drove out of their sight, advancing little more than a few tens of yards east before we came to our first stop: a BP petrol station. We needed to fill up. Then Charley dropped his bike. For the second time that morning.

We looked at each other. We both knew exactly what was running through each other's minds. Had we chosen the wrong bikes? Were they too heavy? Had we overloaded them? And how the hell would we cope with them on the rough roads, swamps, marshes, and deserts of Asia when we couldn't balance them on the flat tarmac of Shepherd's Bush? But the explanation for Charley's sudden weakness was rather less prosaic.

CHARLEY: When it came to saying our last goodbyes, I was shaking with nerves. Ewan had said goodbye to Eve, his daughters and his mother at his home, riding away from them with tears streaming down his face. Fortunately my daughters, Doone and Kinvara, were fairly cool and reserved. I gave them a big hug and told them to look after their mum. Then I kissed Olly and squeezed her tight, holding my emotions in check until I swung my leg over the bike, at which point I overbalanced. Unable to support all that weight, I dropped the bike in front of thirty people. I looked over at Olly and I could see the tears welling up in her eyes – and I lost it. With the help of a few of the onlookers, I hoisted the bike back up and, gritting my teeth, rode away from my family and friends. I was so wobbly I couldn't hold the bike. By the time we reached the petrol station, I had lost all my energy. The emotions involved in leaving my wife and children, and all the domestic hassles we'd had in the last few days, frantically trying to get things done before I left, welled up inside me. I dropped the bike again, smashing the indicator lamp.

Struggling to pull myself together, I still harboured a nagging doubt that we had chosen the wrong bike. I'd always favoured the lighter KTM over the BMW. And now it seemed I might have been right.

Knowing we would face much more demanding terrain, we rode out of the petrol station and down Hammersmith Road with our hearts in our mouths. Approaching Hammersmith roundabout, we stopped beside a white van full of builders. 'Hey, we saw you on TV yesterday,' one of them shouted. 'When are you off?'

'Right now. We're on our way to Folkestone. To the Channel tunnel,' we shouted.

'Good luck!' he yelled, waving his arm. From inside the van came the sound of cheering and his mates roaring: 'We'll follow you in *Motorcycle News*. Have a great time! It's brilliant what you guys are doing! Have a good one!'

For the first time, it dawned on us that we were really on the road. The preparation was over and we were taking off, riding towards the sunrise, two mates on the road together for the next three and a half months. It was a great feeling. We whooped and shouted to one another over the intercom radio, giddy with the feeling of escape. It was a beautiful spring day, the kind you dream about, the sky a brilliant cloudless blue, the air warm and soft. The sixty miles to the coast passed in a blur, as all the way to Folkestone people cheered, waved, tooted their car horns and shouted good luck. The big BMWs were purring beneath us, the first miles were under the wheels and it felt great to be alive.

3 ▶ ▶ ▶

No surprises

LONDON TO UKRAINIAN BORDER

1261

MILES

EWAN: Before we knew it we were boarding the train under the English Channel. I signed some autographs and read some text messages from friends wishing us good luck, and then we were out of the tunnel and riding the autoroute through the flat plains of northern France. It was sweet riding and before we knew it we had crossed the border to Belgium and arrived in Brussels. By early evening, we were ensconced in a hotel and, relieved the first day's riding was behind us, we showered, dressed and hit the town.

Brussels was a surprise. Not the city of Euro bureaucrats and dusty bourgeois burghers it is often said to be, it was like the more laid-back quarters of Paris fifteen years ago, with lots of bars and crowds of young people eating outside. We wandered across pretty squares, soaking up the atmosphere, enjoying the sunshine and looking forward to dinner. Then a policeman pulled up and beckoned us over. 'Hey, you! Come here,' he shouted. 'Yeah, you! Here! You.'

Thinking we had inadvertently done something wrong, we immediately felt guilty and made our way cautiously over to the van.

'Hey! I like your films,' the policeman said. '*Trainshpotting!*' he added. 'Is good, yeah?'

Wandering on for a couple of hours, feeling as if we were on holiday, we stumbled on a square where two middle-aged men were playing jazz – a saxophonist in a beret and his tanned grey-haired accomplice tapping a tambourine. With tables and chairs dotted randomly around the square, the ambience was great. But as soon as we sat down, I wanted a cigarette. Max, a friend who had helped me kick the habit, had warned I had begun making excuses for taking up smoking again even before I had left.

'I'm really hungry, but all I can think about is a cigarette,' I told Charley.

'Would you be able to do it just in the evening? A couple of cigarettes with dinner and then never . . . ?' said Charley, who could confine smoking to a few sociable cigarettes when he had a drink.

'Yeah, yeah, yeah,' I said unconvincingly. 'Yeah . . . probably . . .'

'Shall we have dinner then?' Charley said.

'Let's pretend we've eaten already, then I can have a cigarette now . . . My God, what am I saying? Cigarette today, heroin tomorrow. Reasons? Who needs reasons when you've cigarettes.'

It was the first time in months we'd had time just to chat. No lists to make, no routes to consider, no equipment to think about or bikes to prepare. Then, dog-tired, we headed back to our hotel for a sound night's sleep.

The next day we headed for the Nürburgring in Germany, a mecca for petrolheads forever associated with Niki Lauda's horrific crash in 1976, bringing to an end the Ring's golden days but cementing its reputation as the longest, most beautiful and most challenging Grand Prix racetrack ever built.

With music from our iPods blaring into our helmets, the GPS navigation system relieving us of map-reading tasks and the fabulous weather holding, we entered Germany and soon exited the autobahn on to a beautifully built road leading to the racetrack. It was the kind of road about which bikers dream. Long, sweeping bends and smooth tarmac winding through lightly wooded hills and valleys. It was the kind of road that asked to be taken full pelt and, as we drew up at the Ring's parking lot, I wondered how long it would take Charley to suggest we go out for a burn. Before I even had my helmet off, Charley was bounding over.

'Shall we take these panniers off, buy some tickets and rip around the Ring?' he asked.

'Why don't we get some lunch first?' I replied.

CHARLEY: After lunch, we explored the track, chatting to other bikers, waiting for five o'clock, when the track would be opened to the public.

'Where you going?' several German bikers asked us. 'To Italy?'

'No, to New York,' we said.

'Huh?' . . . 'What?' . . . 'How?' they chorused. It was really quite funny to watch their baffled faces until we explained our route.

EWAN: Just hanging out with nothing to do was a delight. No demands on my time, no phones ringing. It was unreal.

We found a good vantage point on a fast double right-hand bend, but it was purgatory watching other bikers scream past, knowing they had the full run of the Ring's fourteen-plus miles, with its eighty-four right-handers, eighty-eight left-handers, long straights, steep hills and winding track through four villages.

'Look!' I shouted. 'There's someone going around in their people carrier, a dad taking it flat out with his wife in the front and their two children strapped in the back.' The people carrier was being chased by a young lad in a cardigan driving a tiny clapped-out hatchback, careening around the circuit at breakneck speed but driving quite nonchalantly, chatting to his mate in the passenger seat. And then a bike passed by relatively slowly, the rider taking it easy with his girlfriend riding pillion on the back.

'Aaah,' we both shouted. There was something very touching about that biker cautiously circuiting the Ring and it made us both think of our wives and children at home.

But Charley was still fixated on having a go on the track. 'I can feel that track-day sick feeling inside me now,' he said. 'It feels like my gut is dragging me to the bike going

"Come on! Climb on, so we can get on to the track" while I am forcing myself back.'

Placated by a promise that we would return to the Ring for a race day in the autumn, after our circumnavigation, Charley was persuaded not to succumb to temptation. As the sun was setting, we climbed up to Schloss Nürburg, a twelfth-century castle overlooking the circuit. It had, we agreed, been a perfect day. 'God, it's beautiful here, isn't it,' I said to no one in particular.

CHARLEY: The next morning, we decided to ride the 470 miles to Prague in one hit. The idea of an extra day in Prague recuperating appealed to us both.

'I am really apprehensive about getting to Prague,' Ewan said. 'Right now I'm just out on my bike with my best mate on a biking holiday. When we get to Prague, we'll have to meet up with Russ and David to do the filming. That feels just like work to me.'

I felt just the same. I'd had weird anxiety dreams during the night about meeting up with the others, particularly Claudio von Planta, our cameraman. The journey was meant to come first. But if you decide to film a journey, everything about that journey changes because you are filming it. We'd only been on the road for two and a half days, but we were already heartily fed up with filming ourselves. It got in the way of the journey, so the only solution was to have Claudio travel with us permanently. That meant an end to our dream of two mates on the road alone.

We hardly noticed the last few miles on German soil, riding through the Bavarian Forest to the Czech frontier. It was only when we drew up beside a Czech border guard that we realised we were leaving behind the ordered security of western Europe. 'This is giving me the heebie-jeebies,' I shouted over the radio shortly after we crossed into the Czech Republic.

'Me too,' Ewan replied. 'I guess it's because the unknown starts now.' Despite our best efforts to learn Russian, we hadn't advanced beyond a few basic phrases. And as for Czech, Ukrainian, Kazakh and Mongolian, we couldn't speak a word.

Having ridden 470 miles since leaving the Nürburgring, we were tired. Although the BMW made few physical demands, the riding was mentally exhausting and the trek through the suburbs of Prague dragged on like the final hours of a long-haul flight, until we found ourselves crossing an ornate road bridge into the city, a magnificent view of the spires of Prague spanning the opposite riverbank and on a hill above us a massive monument with a ticking arm. And all of it washed in the light from the blood-red sun. It was a stunning entrance.

That evening we met up with Russ, David, Claudio and Jim Simak, the second unit cameraman, and the next day we took to the streets of Prague. We were staggered by its

beauty. Wandering across the bridges that spanned the winding Vltava River, climbing up towards Hradcany Castle and exploring the narrow streets and baroque buildings of the old quarter, we were like any other tourists – albeit tourists with two cameramen constantly in tow. And like thousands of visitors to Prague, we sat on the Charles Bridge while an artist sketched us in caricature, watching the world go by, although we briefly became a tourist attraction ourselves as dozens of passers-by stopped to snap Ewan with their cameras and mobile phones.

But as the day went on it became apparent that our sightseeing route had been chosen by Russ and David to suit their planned filming opportunities. The caricatures on Charles Bridge, it turned out, had been set up. Then came a visit to Parvina, a gypsy Russ had briefed to tell our fortunes. A dark-haired middle-aged woman in a housecoat, Parvina dealt some tarot cards. Pointing to a card labelled The Lady, which appeared every time she dealt the tarot deck, the gypsy told Ewan he would meet a significant person on the trip. But she also said he would meet someone who would double-cross him. It could be someone you know already, she warned him. My tarot revealed little, merely that I had a long journey ahead and that I was missing my family. Hardly revelations from the other side.

After the tarot reading, we made it clear to Russ and David that we wanted no more set-ups. We'd prefer it if from now on we let the journey dictate the filming, we said, and not the other way round.

'Yeah, yeah, absolutely. Whatever you guys want, we'll do it,' David reassured us. 'From now on, no surprises, no set-ups.'

'In the spirit of no surprises . . .' David began – we were discussing what to do that evening – 'we've arranged for you to eat at a medieval restaurant in the centre of Prague and we've got a few things for you to do.'

'And what might those things be?' Ewan asked.

'Don't worry,' Russ said, 'you'll be totally cool with it.'

EWAN: With period music, a contrived menu and the waiting staff dressed in period costumes, this was the kind of theme restaurant from which we would normally run a mile. We sat around, feeling like a bunch of gormless goons. David and Russ persuaded me to try on a male chastity belt, then, after the main courses, they announced that they'd arranged with the chef for us to cook a traditional pudding, a medieval pancake. Under the chef's instruction, we made up some batter and threw it into a frying pan, but with the chef and kitchen staff gazing at us with a mixture of amusement, disbelief and contempt, we found it impossible to muster enthusiasm for the sorry charade.

'This is really cool,' David said. 'We could do around the world in ten local dishes.'

He had really not got the plot. Christ! If this was the kind of thing they were going to organise, this trip was going to be a disaster. Unable to see a way forward, neither of us slept well that night.

The next morning, as we were getting our bikes ready, I approached David. 'These set-up things and your surprises are just not going to work,' I said. 'Learning how to make a medieval omelette – or whatever that pancake was – was pants. It just proved to Charley and me that your set-ups just aren't going to work.'

I was seriously worried. If we didn't sort out things now the spirit of the journey would be lost. We knew relations wouldn't always be this strained because we'd been through a lot together to get this far. But now we desperately needed to remind ourselves of our original vision.

CHARLEY: We set off in convoy, riding for about two hours behind Russ and David in their Mitsubishi 4×4s from Prague to near the Slovak border, stopping at a Cistercian monastery in Sedlec to visit the All Saints chapel. Built in the fifteenth century and known as the Kostnice, the Ossuary or the Beinhaus, the latter a typically pragmatic German word meaning the bone house, this ghoulish place contained the skeletons of more than forty

Puppets for sale on the streets of Prague.

thousand people. In the late thirteenth century, King Otakar II of Bohemia sent Henry, the abbot of Sedlec, on a diplomatic mission to the Holy Land. Henry brought back a handful of earth from Golgotha, the hill upon which Jesus is believed to have been crucified. Sprinkling it over the monastery cemetery, he transformed it into the most desirable graveyard in central Europe. A succession of plagues, the Hussite wars, and an enormous demand for burial plots from the wealthy filled the cemetery with tens of thousands of graves and the bones began to pile up.

In the early fifteenth century a church was built in the middle of the cemetery and a half-blind Cistercian monk assigned the task of stacking a chapel beneath it with bones exhumed from earlier graves. Then, in 1870, František Rint, a local woodcarver, began turning the bones into a macabre work of art. The centrepiece is a chandelier comprising every bone in the human body. Huge arrangements of bones in the shapes of bells hang in each corner of the chapel. A coat of arms and various ornaments, all made entirely from bones, fill the chapel.

EWAN: As we walked around the chapel in our motorbike kit, staring at the eerie display, I thought it was the most gruesome and chilling thing I'd ever seen, though actually quite beautiful and I don't know why, but it was just a bit cheesy, even if it was made out of people's bones. It was like a serial killer's wet dream in that chapel and it put me right off my lunch.

CHARLEY: After the Bone Church, we headed off on our own with Claudio.

We stopped off for lunch in a beautiful medieval square that could have been a set from Disneyland. We walked around, gazing at the painted shop fronts, stopping to look at market stalls and a beautiful fountain in the centre, while Claudio quietly got on with the filming. Within a few minutes we had the whole thing in the bag. It was such a relief to discover that between the three of us we could get it done without any fuss.

From the square we rode for several hours through a valley with a river flowing beside a road lined with cliff walls and dotted with abandoned factories and industrial plants, until we started climbing to the Punkva Caves at the Pusty zleb in the Moravian Karst, a wild mountainous area north of Brno. With more than a thousand caves, the region has been designated a World Heritage site. And if there's one reason to come to the Czech Republic, it's to come and see these caves. They're really quite something.

We hopped into a boat and entered the caves with the whole place to ourselves because we had arrived late in the day. We spent about an hour exploring a maze of stalagmites and stalactites, open-mouthed at the scale and beauty of it all. While the guide explained that the caves were three hundred million years old and that the stalagmites grew by one millimetre every thirty years, we walked deep into the mountain, through a door, down a short path and then into the most incredible gorge. It was immense, with green moss and algae everywhere and even patches of snow because it had its own microclimate. On the far right, a river emerged from a cliff into a large lake. We just looked at it in silence for several minutes, bowled over by it all, our arms around each other, soaking it all in.

After a night in a traveller's hotel in a small village, we rendezvoused with the support team at the Slovakian border. Even before we got off our bikes, Russ ran over to speak to us.

'Did you get your carnet stamped on the way in?' he yelled.

'No,' I said.

'You really didn't? Do you know how important that carnet is?'

'We're only travellers,' I replied. 'Surely if we can enter the country without stamping the carnet, we can do the same when we leave it.'

'You can't, mate. The carnet's a bond kinda thing. You can't play around with the rules. Believe me, mate, you can't do that to these things.'

Russ was in a state of panic.

Everything had been so sweet and so smooth until we met up with the crew. Suddenly we were embroiled in a massive drama at the border, a place where we needed to keep a low profile. We hadn't stamped our carnet coming into the Czech Republic, which we needed to prove we hadn't sold any of our equipment. If anyone had told us we'd need it, we'd forgotten.

'Listen,' I said. 'Just calm down. You're getting really worked up about this when we need to keep our cool. Just calm down.'

Russ lost it altogether. 'You deal with it,' he snapped and stomped off.

Eventually we got it sorted. We paid a small fee for not having stamped our carnet and that was that. Fifteen minutes later, we were in Slovakia. What a faff about nothing.

EWAN: We stopped for lunch at a roadhouse near Bojnice. I chased a great big hairy spider off my tank bag, which I took to be a sign of good luck, wrote some postcards and just enjoyed being with Charley and Claudio.

After lunch we got out our cigarettes – I was back on twenty a day – and planned our journey ahead. We stopped at a castle near Bojnice, where we were surprised to bump into some English tourists, particularly when their daughter pulled out a *Down With Love* DVD and asked me to sign it. Then we booked into a hotel in the town, on the way to where the parents of Claudio's children's nanny lived.

CHARLEY: We left the hotel early, riding through the Slovakian countryside, at times in heavy rain. On two occasions we came upon motorcyclists waiting for us. They were sitting on the side of the road and, as we passed them, we waved. They immediately put on their helmets and chased after us. At the next traffic lights, they stopped beside us for a chat. It seemed very strange, but also very charming, that motorcyclists who had read about our journey now went out of their way to join us for a few miles.

We rode through villages and towns which were completely deserted, ghost towns built around a factory that had long been abandoned. Where we did chance upon a few people, they all stopped what they were doing as we approached, staring at us as we passed by.

'It's as if we were from the moon,' Ewan said over the radio. At one point, we came around a bend, emerged from some woods and it was as if the world had dropped away on one side of the road. To our right was the most magnificent view, valleys and mountains stretching away from us for tens of miles.

Late in the evening we arrived at Turna Nad Bodvou, a small town in a valley dominated by a massive cement factory, and were led by Claudio to the house where the parents of his children's nanny lived. It was a large terraced house backed by a garden overflowing with vegetables. Csaba Kaposztas looked like a silver-haired Jack Nicholson and Maria, his wife, had a beaming smile and spoke excellent English. 'I learned it at school,' she said, 'but I never got the chance to travel and to use it.'

Completely self-sufficient, keeping chickens and a pig to make their own sausages and ham, they were an amazing couple. 'It's lovely to be in this home,' Ewan said. 'It's such a nice welcome difference.'

Maria cooked a traditional Slovakian dinner of spicy tomato soup with paprika, pork from one of their own pigs and cake. 'It's my husband's favourite,' she said. 'Eat plenty of it. Breakfast isn't until the morning.'

'A good philosophy,' Ewan replied.

As we ate, Maria showed us pictures of her family and told us about her seventy-year-old pen pal in Edinburgh. They had been writing to each other for thirty years but had never met.

After dinner, Csaba led us into the garage. Pushing his Lada towards the door, he uncovered a flight of steps beneath it. At the bottom we squeezed through a small gap chiselled through the concrete and entered a vast space that this most resourceful of men had hollowed out underneath his home. Along each wall, oak wine barrels were decorated with medals he had won for the wine he made from his own vines.

But that wasn't all. The vault was lined with bottles of homemade fruit and grain schnapps, brandy and apple brandy, all offered for tasting.

'Jesus,' Ewan whispered to me. 'If you lit a match down here, the whole fucking country would blow up.'

The next morning, after breakfast, Maria and Csaba took us on a tour of the village by car, proudly pointing out the frescos in the church and indicating derelict buildings, their windows and frames apparently stolen by gypsies.

'Slovaks work hard and want to make the country better,' Csaba said, his wife translating. 'But gypsies just play music and dance and want to do nothing.' Ewan and I looked at each other. It was depressing to see travellers facing the same intolerance in central Europe as at home.

We eventually bade them farewell and pressed on for the border. Several hours later, having taken two hours to cross the Slovak frontier, we were waiting to cross the Ukrainian border when Russ ran up with a message from Sergey, our Russian fixer.

'Right. Here's the deal. The customs officials will only accept original vehicle registration documents, but we only have photocopies. BMW and Mitsubishi have the originals. If we can't get through here, our only alternative is to turn back and head north into Poland, through Belarus and Russia to Kazakhstan.'

We were sticky and dirty and the sun was beating down. Needing to get away from the others to figure a way out of our dilemma, I ambled across to a shabby toilet block and bumped into an old Slovak who spoke a few words of German, a language of which I also had only a rudimentary grasp.

'*Ukraine nicht gut. Grosse Mafia. Viele probleme*,' the old man warned urgently. Holding up two fingers like a gun, he emphasised his point. 'Peng, peng,' he said, shooting in the air with his fingers. '*Mafia alles Ukraine.*'

There was no mistaking the sincerity of his warning. The Ukraine was clearly not a place a bunch of expensively kitted-out and obviously wealthy Western motorcyclists should consider visiting. I wandered back and told Ewan the bad news.

'Everyone stay calm and we'll be all right. Don't panic. Those mafia guys can smell fear,' he said.

'But the old man said they'll steal everything, then kill you,' I whimpered.

Fixing me with a cold stare, Ewan sucked on his cigarette, exhaled and sighed: 'So what the fuck are we going to do?'

As we soon found out, border crossings could be slow and frustrating, but always a great chance to meet the local people.

4 ▶▶▶

► ► ►

Little by little

ACROSS THE UKRAINE

1341

CHARLEY: I spotted him shortly after midnight. I was tired, irritable and desperate to cross the frontier after negotiating with guards and officials for eleven hours. I wanted more than anything just to be able to crawl into bed. Then I noticed him watching me.

About forty, he looked like a successful businessman, but his BMW had red number plates. Diplomatic plates. And he knew all the guards, policemen and functionaries. Chatting to the guards beneath the fluorescent lighting above the customs huts, he would occasionally stare at our small group. I was standing near Russ and David in the darkness; Ewan was wrapped in his sleeping bag on a patch of scrubland, trying to sleep while trucks belched diesel fumes around him. The Ukrainian businessman called up a Toyota that had been ransacked for drugs or some other contraband, I assumed, and, turning to me, he shrugged.

I shrugged back. 'Pffft,' I said, hoping the universal expression for 'What the hell can you do?' meant the same thing in the Ukraine.

'Yeah,' he said in heavily accented English. 'Import cheaper.'

I went back to discussing with Russ the only real subject of interest. Where were we going to sleep that night?

'I have a hotel.' It was the businessman. 'Camelot. Why don't you come and stay? Have dinner. Parking no problem. Garages no problem.'

There was nothing to suggest this businessman was a gangster. But if you owned a big hotel in the Ukraine, you would certainly be paying protection money. I strolled over to Ewan and told him about the offer.

'Why is this guy prepared to hang around for ages to help out a bunch of strangers?' Ewan asked. It was a good point. And if we ignored it we would be disregarding the first lesson of our training for surviving in a hostile environment.

EWAN: Jamie Lowther-Pinkerton, now Private Secretary to Princes William and Harry, could have stepped out of the textbook for English army officers. Tall, skinny, patrician and quietly authoritative, he ran a three-day course on hostile environments. He trained business executives, journalists, voluntary workers and government officials bound for the most dangerous places on earth, including war zones.

Jamie, we now know for definite, was a former member of the SAS, although he never confirmed it to us and changed the subject whenever special forces were mentioned.

'What does SAS actually mean?' Charley asked.

'Special Air Service,' I interjected, hoping Jamie might open up.

'Oh . . . yeah . . . er . . . Special Air Service . . . yeah . . . isn't it?' Jamie said in the faltering way he used to deflect inquiries. 'Yeah . . . or Scandinavian Air Services . . .'

'It doesn't really feel right,' Ewan said. 'I can't stop thinking what's in it for him and wondering what we are letting ourselves in for.'

Roman woke up his staff and insisted they cook us dinner. At four in the morning, we sat down for a three-course feast in his basement nightclub decorated like a dungeon but decked out instead with spinning glitterballs, flashing strobes and a psychedelic lightshow.

'This must be a one-off,' I said to Sergey. 'It's so wonderfully kitsch.'

'No, no, no,' he said, 'this is quite normal for Russia or the Ukraine.'

Russ, who had had a few vodkas, was all for celebrating crossing the border. But, still nervous about being bumped off in the night, I sloped off to bed. Back in the room, I scanned the light fittings and the pictures on the wall for hidden cameras, but found nothing. Then I opened a cupboard. There in front of me was a shoe-shine pack. The building was a hotel after all. Feeling guilty for being so suspicious, I switched on the television, watched it for a few minutes and dropped off to sleep in the armchair. Rest at last.

EWAN: I woke early and went outside. In the cold light of day, I could see that what in the wee hours of the morning had seemed such a vividly scary mafia hideout, where gangsters were going to slit our throats and take our money, was nothing more than a very innocent hotel. Maybe living in London had made me wary of strangers. It was a habit I wanted to shake off.

Wandering through the empty hotel while Charley and the rest of the team slept, I came across a map of the world on a wall. It took my breath away. Compared with what lay ahead, we had travelled so little. But the moment my mind drifted to the bigger picture, that we'd reach Russia in a few days, the journey became overwhelming and panic set in.

Every mile took us further away from home, further away from our families, and increasingly I felt the loneliness of not being with my wife. But accompanying the moments that tugged at our heartstrings there were times of great wonder, flashes of magic. Like when we were riding at the end of the day and the sun, setting in the west, warmed our backs and threw our shadows ahead of us on the road. Just chasing our shadows as we headed east. All the way round the world to get home.

The magic continued when we set off that morning. Western Ukraine was a deeply agricultural country with small villages, farms, horses pulling ploughs and lots of women working on the land, while the men seemed to have nothing better to do than sit at the side of the road. The Ukrainians appeared to have spent all their money putting up mobile phone masts and had forgotten the roads, but it was nothing the bikes couldn't cope with. Then came a call over the radio. It was David: 'We're approaching our first bit of drama.'

At the edge of a village, a barrier had been pulled down across the road. A guard was standing beside a hut. We didn't know if he was a policeman, a soldier, a government official or a local bandit.

'They just want to see our papers,' Sergey said. 'It will be okay.'

It was local police. They wanted to see our vehicle registration documents, and photocopies would not do. It had to be the originals. We sat at the edge of the road, smoking to pass the time, waiting for something to break the impasse.

'You want to know what I think?' Vasiliy said in his thick Russian accent. 'Nobody promised us this trip would be easy. But it will be okay. You have to be patient.'

While Ukrainian trucks, coaches and cranes passed through the checkpoint, we waited and explored the village. There were old peasant women, their heads wrapped in scarves, clutching babies. Children were drawing water from a well.

A grocer's shop was well stocked with basic provisions, giving us a chance to exercise the few words of Russian we had learned during the months of preparation. By smiling and pointing we managed to buy a few groceries.

The housewives in the shop asked us where we were from. '*Ingliski*,' we said. They gabbled back in Ukrainian. '*Russki*' was not good, they made clear.

This unplanned stopover had been the highlight of the trip so far. Unencumbered by the trappings of celebrity, at last I was meeting real people in their own surroundings. I took myself over to a well and sat down on the edge of it. A little old lady came out of her rickety wooden house and joined me; she fed her cat and started to chat in Ukrainian. I couldn't understand what she was saying but it didn't seem to matter. I just listened to her voice and then I told her about us.

She touched my forehead and crossed herself several times. I got the impression she was saying that I'd been sent to meet her, but there was no way to know for sure. I think she was trying to tell me about her life, talking about the war and how terrible it had been. At one point she said she would pray for me. I told her we were going a very long way and that it would be very nice if she prayed for us. It was beautiful and I'll never forget her. She really touched me. She was a gorgeous woman, with beautiful eyes. I was really disappointed when I heard that at last we'd been let through the checkpoint.

Ewan with a Ukrainian woman. They managed to have
a long conversation despite the language barrier.

CHARLEY: We continued on through western Ukraine, bound for Lviv. It looked incredibly poor and indeed some of the Ukrainians were ploughing the fields by hand. It was a pitiful existence and the whole landscape looked black and white. No colour. Nothing. The poverty was staggering, particularly as it seemed so close to home. It had taken us only a week to reach the Ukraine, yet it was another world.

By the evening we had reached Lviv, another long day's riding of more than 160 miles on broken roads. At the hotel, Claudio asked where we could park our bikes safely and the manager said 'here', pointing to the foyer of his slightly down-at-heel palace of an hotel. Ewan rolled back the carpets and we rode the bikes up a couple of stairs, through the double doors into the lavishly decorated hall, laughing at the ridiculousness of trying to turn the heavy bikes around on the slippery polished marble floor.

We washed, changed and walked around the city with Andrej Hunyak, a Ukrainian friend of Claudio's. Lviv was a beautiful place. Classical buildings, big squares with old men playing chess, most of the roads cobbled and uneven. Over dinner, we asked Andrej about the change from communism to democracy. 'It was pretty dodgy,' he said. 'All you could get was the bare necessities. Now we've got plenty on the shelves but we haven't got money to buy it.'

We'd heard similar stories in most of eastern Europe. Many people in the Ukraine spoke at length about the mafia but nobody would let us use this in the documentary. It was a potent indication of the hold the mafia had over Ukrainians and their country.

EWAN: Facing a tough deadline, we left the hotel early the next morning. Three hundred and sixty miles to ride by three o'clock. We had an appointment in Kiev at a Unicef centre that looked after children affected by the Chernobyl disaster.

We stopped for coffee at a kiosk beneath a massive Soviet-era communist sculpture of a clenched fist thrusting out from the side of a hill. As I pulled my bike around to the kiosk, I noticed I was doing a U-turn in the road around what had once been a dog. It had been hit so hard that it had exploded all over the road. It was by far the worst road kill I'd ever seen.

What do you do when you don't have secure parking?
In Lviv our hotel manager pulled up the carpets and let us park our bikes in the lobby.

Charley and I stood sipping our coffee in silence while Claudio filmed the sculpture. It was the first time since leaving London that we'd not had anything to say to each other and our introspection had been exacerbated by getting used to riding with Claudio since Prague.

We'd all seen the dog, but no one had dared mention it. 'That dog's all over the place,' I eventually said quietly. Charley looked at me and we both cracked up. 'It doesn't know its arse from its elbow,' I added and we fell into a fit of giggles. It was in such poor taste, but just what was needed to break the heavy silence.

'You know what was the last thing that went through that dog's mind?' Charley said. 'Its arse.'

For the next few minutes, we trotted out one bad pun after another, grimacing as passing trucks squished and splattered the poor dog flatter into the road.

'Nooooo, don't watch,' Charley shouted each time it was run over again, but we were in hysterics. The dark mood had been broken. Charley and I were back in good shape.

The Chernobyl Children's Project was housed in a slightly dilapidated four-storey building that had been set aside for children who had suffered from the effects of the nuclear disaster in 1986. The centre was set up by Katernya Novak, a remarkable woman who lived less than a mile from the edge of the nuclear power station complex in Pripyat. After the fire broke out and the radiation escaped her first reaction was to help children like her own whose health had been damaged by the accident. Many had thyroid cancers or leukaemia.

The children at the Chernobyl centre were fantastic and we were thrilled to be there and to be involved with Unicef. One of the great honours that comes along with doing the job I do is that you can be involved in raising awareness for charities or helping them raise money. I don't care what anybody says: there's no harm in it. I was extremely pleased to have built a link with Unicef that I hoped to carry on.

CHARLEY: The next day we took the bikes for their first service and went sightseeing. Kiev was beautiful. Unspoilt, laid-back and the first city we'd stopped in where Ewan didn't feel hassled. Browsing through a flea market, we stopped to look at a stall selling fur hats.

'Do I know you?' It was one of the market traders, young and wearing a pair of wraparound shades.

'Yes. Maybe you know me. This is Charley,' Ewan said, swinging his arm around the stallholder and slapping him on the back.

'Welcome to the Ukraine. Are you on the bikes?'

'Yes, we are,' Ewan said. 'How did you know about that?'

**Visiting the dedicated staff and amazing children at
The Chernobyl Children's Project with Unicef.**

'Am I looking like I am stupid? I saw the TV. Two BMWs, right?'

Then another stallholder wandered over. 'How you doing . . . Ewan McGregor?'

'Yes. How are you? Good to see you.'

'I watched your movie. *Big Fish*. Not your best one. You want to buy something? I make a special price, guys . . .'

The market was an eye-opener. Caviar was being sold by the bucketload and the streets were thronged with big Mercedes and BMWs driven by shifty-looking flash geezers, invariably with a very pretty, expensively dressed girl in $500 shades sitting beside them.

We stopped for lunch – Chicken Kiev, of course. Then we visited a Soviet-era monument in a public park, a place of pilgrimage for newlyweds. Dressed in their white dresses and tuxedos, they were having their pictures taken beneath the arched monument.

'These Soviet statues and pieces of art really do inspire a kind of awe,' Ewan said. 'They must have given the common man a huge sense of strength and pride.'

But the day was overshadowed by a series of arguments I had with Russ and David. My friend Fred Grolsh, who had recently moved to Kiev, had organised a sightseeing tour

and booked our hotel, but the team were treating him with disdain. At least, so I thought. David and Russ were constantly late, they kept changing their minds, they kept talking over each other and they wouldn't commit to anything. 'Could you just stop and listen to what Fred has got to say and then we can get on with looking around Kiev,' I snapped at David. He said nothing, but it happened again when we dropped off the bikes at the BMW garage and I laid into David.

'Don't you dare show me up in front of someone else,' David snarled at me.

'Well, you fucking listen to my friend who's trying to organise something,' I barked back.

Ewan stepped in. He was very upset. 'You've got to sort out this problem between you, Russ and David,' he said. 'Otherwise it's going to ruin the whole trip.'

I tried apologising to David, but he was having none of it. 'What's the point of saying you're sorry, when you know you're going to do it again?' he said.

That evening, concerned that Russ, David and I were facing a personality clash that could bring an end to the adventure, I sat and thought about it. I realised I was constantly jumping down Russ and David's throats, not letting them finish sentences and telling them what to do even when they knew better. It was a huge turning point. I realised Russ was just being Russ and Dave was just being Dave – I was the one with a problem.

At the root of it, I hadn't faced up to the fact that I would be away from home for such a long time. I missed my children more than I had ever imagined I would and I missed my wife, just cuddling up to her at the end of a day and having a proper chat. It was made worse by my constant worrying each and every day over where we were going to sleep, where we were going to go and what we would do when we got there. I needed to recognise that while Russ and David had their faults, they had done a fantastic job. They'd given their all to our trip and sadly the frictions were mostly my fault. I was trying to control everything when I needed just to let things happen. Otherwise these 108 days were going to slip by and I would have missed it all.

EWAN: Charley and I set off the next morning on our own. Claudio had flown to London to retake his motorcycle test. The BMW was running like a dream and I was heading for Russia. I was happy as old Larry. I loved being on my bike. I loved being on the road.

The only impediment to our progress was the police. We rarely rode for more than half an hour without being stopped, mainly because they wanted to have a look at the bikes. But the third time it happened, when Charley was overtaking, though not at speed, was not so lucky.

5 ▶ ▶ ▶

▶ ▶ ▶

Mansion on the hill

ANTRATSYT

2118

MILES

CHARLEY: The big steel gates to the road swung closed and Igor, the dude with the BMW, introduced us to Gala, his wife, his teenage daughter and some of the other people standing around, and explained how he came to be there.

'So you were on the ships?' I said. 'A seaman.'

'I'm three years submarines and twelve years seaman, industrial fisherman. Soviet Union Atlantic patrol,' he said as he ushered us up to a large attic room where Vladimir, our policeman friend, explained he had brought us to Igor after his wife had said we couldn't stay at his house.

'You sleep here. All your room,' Igor said. It was an impressive space that occupied the entire third floor of the house. There were a few pieces of furniture, some easy chairs and a chest of drawers, and, hanging from its strap in the corner, a machine gun.

'Great Voor,' Igor said proudly, pointing at the tommy-gun. 'Great Voor . . . two!' He pulled back the bolt and squeezed the trigger. The gun gave a clunk then a click. Ewan and I let out sighs of relief. It wasn't loaded.

Igor smiled and nodded. 'Partisans,' he said. 'Russian freedom fighters.'

EWAN: We changed, showered and went downstairs, where Igor was holding court in the large whitewashed kitchen. 'Sit down,' Igor said. Wine, coffee and water were poured and photographs handed round as Igor recounted tales of his life aboard a Soviet submarine. All of the photos were of Igor. And in all of them he was holding a gun.

While Gala cooked, Igor explained his past. He had been a turbine mechanic on the Atlantic submarine patrols from 1981 to 1984. For three months at a time he was incarcerated in a nuclear submarine fitted with a top-secret sonar system, patrolling the Atlantic at the height of the Cold War. Then he joined the merchant navy, working for fifteen years in the Soviet fishing fleet. At some point, he'd been a miner and there had also been a year's unemployment when he first came back home.

Another picture showed Igor in a band. 'Much drunk,' he laughed. 'Soviets . . .' he added as if no other explanation was necessary. Then Igor showed us a photograph of himself standing in front of a Soviet propaganda poster. A gorilla-like American soldier was charging out of the picture, his bayoneted rifle thrust in front of him and his teeth gritted, yelling as he stamped on a globe of the world. 'Crazy times,' Igor shrugged.

At that moment, the doorbell rang. Sitting with my back to the dark wood door, I turned around to be confronted by a broad, tough-looking man. He had a sleepy eye and swollen bruiser's hands, one of which he was offering to me. We shook hands. 'Vladimir,' he said, his deep voice booming.

'Ewan,' I replied, trying not to gulp. I turned back to the room. Charley was sitting opposite me, his eyes widening, pupils dilating as he stared over my shoulder.

'He's taking off his gun,' Charley whispered. I sat absolutely still. More men arrived, all with bulges under their jackets or sweaters. Menacing men who were on best behaviour in Igor's house. Vladimir sat down and cracked the seal on a bottle of vodka.

'We could show you around tomorrow,' he said. 'We could go hunting. You like to hunt? Or we could take you down a coal mine. I work in the mine . . .'

'Yes, you must stay here for two days,' Igor interjected. 'You must see the mine.'

I just wanted to get the fuck out of that house.

We were surrounded by tooled-up men who said they worked in the coal industry, but why would a miner carry a gun? And why was Igor's house so big in a neighbourhood of shacks and small houses?

'So you used to be a sailor, Igor,' Charley said. 'What do you do now?'

'I sell electrical appliances. Kettles. Fridges.' Judging by the mansion and its swimming pool, it must have been an extremely successful business.

'Do you know Madonna?' Gala asked.

'Erm, sorry to disappoint you,' I said, 'but no, I don't.'

Hollywood was mentioned several times. So was *Moulin Rouge*, and gradually I realised that maybe we weren't in quite as much danger as I had initially thought. Igor sat down at the table.

'Why you do this journey?' he asked. 'What for? Who for?'

'It's just to go round the world,' I said. 'To meet other people. Like you.'

'You are interested in travel? You find it interesting?' Igor was perplexed.

'Yes, very interesting.'

'For me, there is nothing interesting in travel. I have done it enough.'

'You come to coal mine tomorrow.' It was Vladimir, becoming more insistent with every glass of vodka.

'We'll see what our producers suggest,' Charley said.

'Have you spoken to them? How will your friends find house?' said Vladimir.

Igor cut in.

'Everybody knows how to find this place,' he said with a flamboyant smile. 'It's mafia centre of town. Everyone knows how to find mafia house.' There was a brief silence and then the room filled with raucous laughter while Charley and I stared at each other, trying hard not to show our nerves. 'We're just kidding,' Igor said. 'Just kidding.'

'And he,' Igor added, pointing at a hard nut with the shaved head and the gun poking out from beneath his sweater, 'he is in Ukrainian anti-terrorist squad.'

The laughter stopped.

At Igor's house in Antratsyt. Igor is on Charley's right, and Vladimir is seated at the front. Large selection of guns not pictured.

Just as the tension was becoming too much to bear, there was a loud knock at the door and David walked in. Charley and I leapt up and threw our arms around them, relieved to see Sergey, Vasiliy, Jim and David. We followed them outside to where the trucks were standing in the drive. While helping them unload, we briefed them on what had gone on. 'You won't believe it,' Charley said to David. 'Igor's fucking amazing. And there are guns everywhere.' David just stared back as if to say: what have you let yourselves in for?

Then we went inside where Igor's wife had set up a huge dining table in the hallway, laden with bottles of vodka, bowls of rice, chicken and lamb, and a baked cheese dish. Much of the dinner was spent chinking glasses and throwing back shots of vodka, or in my case, water. The hospitality was overwhelming. More people arrived, most of them men and all wanting to shake our hands and to examine the bikes in the garage.

Dinner over, only a few of us remained in the kitchen, chatting and drinking. Charley, Vladimir, our doctor Vasiliy and a bunch of heavies were outside. Igor was nowhere to be seen. Hearing footsteps behind me, I turned around. My heart skipped a beat. Igor was coming down the stairs, laughing manically, a guitar held aloft in his left hand and a Kalashnikov in his right. David had frozen in mid-movement, his mouth open wide.

Igor swung the Kalashnikov around, snapping out the stock with a loud, metallic twanging sound. 'Ffffbbbbing' it went.

'I'd enjoyed meeting people along the road and I'd been blown away by the helpfulness of complete strangers.'

EWAN

The room reverberated with a twang as the butt of the gun snapped into place, a sound I will never forget. Grinning wildly, Igor cocked the machine gun, shouted 'Please! Please!' and squeezed the trigger. I felt my guts churn. The gun clicked. The chamber, as far as I could tell, was empty. Or would the bullet follow with the next click?

'Welcome! Welcome!' Igor boomed. We all laughed nervously. 'Here!'

And then I found myself with the machine gun in my hands. Sergey gently took it from me, glanced in the magazine and peered down the barrel, and, satisfied they were empty, handed it back.

'Oh yeah . . . oh yeah . . . made in Russia . . . nice . . . that's a nice gun,' I said, stuck for words. After all, what do you say to someone who's just come downstairs brandishing a Kalashnikov?

Pap! Pap! Pap! Pap! Four gunshots cracked in the garage just outside the kitchen door, the garage that Charley had entered less than a minute earlier.

'Oh my God,' I whispered. David was as white as a sheet. Telling myself Charley would be all right, I wandered as casually as I could out to the garage.

CHARLEY: Brandishing a Kalashnikov, Ewan burst out of the kitchen door, closely followed by David. For a split second, I thought everything was about to go horribly wrong: the heavies would assume Ewan, having heard the gunshots, had imagined I'd been wasted and had seized a loaded machine gun to shoot his way out of the compound.

Ewan, spotting me healthy and alive, immediately relaxed. But David looked like a cornered animal. 'Charley, my heart stopped beating,' he said, throwing his arms around me. 'I thought you'd been fucking blootered.'

We'd been standing outside the garage, just by the kitchen door, and Vladimir and some of the heavies had been showing off their guns. 'That's not a gun,' Vladimir had said, pointing at one of his associate's weapons and pulling his pistol out of its holster. Doof! Doof! Doof! Doof! He fired four rounds in the air. To them it was innocent fun, but to us it was more telling than anything we'd seen so far – Igor and his friends clearly didn't need to worry about letting off their guns in a built-up neighbourhood.

One of the things that had slightly worried me before we set out was that maybe nothing much would happen.

'It's insane, man,' Ewan said, a broad smile cracking his face. 'We had dinner, usually people then bring in some coffee, but Igor brought in a fucking machine gun.'

EWAN: We went back inside to find Igor standing halfway up the stairs. Lifting his left foot up one step, he stood askew, his guitar clutched to his chest. He then launched into the most dramatic folk song imaginable, clicking his fingers, plucking the strings, then strumming them manically. It was a *tour de force*.

I admired him for his chutzpah, his love of life and his hospitality. But at the same time he scared me to death. Afterwards, Charley and I went outside for a cigarette. We could hear Igor still singing inside. 'I'm feeling really good,' I said. 'On the one hand there's an element of not knowing what the fuck is going on, but at this point I don't know if that's because of me or them.'

'They're being incredibly friendly,' Charley said. 'I think they genuinely want to show us around tomorrow and I don't think we should miss the chance.'

Charley and I watched our warm breath condensing in the cold night air. 'It really is freezing,' Charley said. 'Look, I've got goose pimples.'

'My mum would die if she could see us now. Out in T-shirts on a cold night and, behind us, a house jammed to the rafters with guns,' I said. 'She wouldn't sleep for months if she knew!'

The next morning I wanted to get on the move, but Charley thought the mine visit was an opportunity we shouldn't pass up. 'We need to leave at midday,' Charley told Igor. 'If we can visit the mine and get away before noon, then fine.'

'Let's go,' Igor said. 'You ride in my car.'

The mine was much larger than I had expected. It had dozens of buildings, several mineshafts and a web of conveyor belts crisscrossing the complex. Vladimir, the vodka king, was waiting to take us on a tour.

CHARLEY: Vladimir took us to a tiled locker room and handed us miners' outfits. White linen long johns and vest, dark gabardine jacket and trousers, Wellington boots and a helmet. 'Just so that they don't get blood on our clothes when they cap us downstairs,' Ewan joked.

Down the mine in Antratsyt. With no ventilation, we were left completely drained after forty minutes, yet the miners endured six-hour shifts in the same conditions.

Instead of a lift, the mine had a cage on rails that descended a very steep incline for almost a mile to the coal face. 'Imagine my agent now,' Ewan yelled as the driver released the brake. 'If she could see me . . .' The cage plummeted into the earth with a roar which sounded like the afterburners on a fighter jet engine. We hung on for dear life and six minutes later we came to a shuddering halt.

Underground, the pit was staggeringly primitive. Packs of a dozen men were pushing ten-ton trucks of coal along railway lines. There was no lighting except for the lamps on the miners' helmets. All around, tunnel walls had crumbled and their roofs collapsed. In western Europe, the mine would have been condemned. With no ventilation, the lack of oxygen left us completely drained after a mere forty minutes, yet the miners endured six-hour shifts in the same conditions. An unbelievable, overwhelming glimpse into a very different world.

EWAN: Back at Igor's house, Gala had made lunch. Again a massive spread. Again a lot of heavies hanging around. And again a long series of vodka toasts. One of the heavies from the previous night turned up. A judo and karate fanatic who pulled two beautiful necklaces from beneath his clothes and gave them to Charley and me.

'This for you,' he said in broken English. 'This to give you good luck because your journey is so great, so big.'

Every family member, friend and associate of Igor had to be hugged and kissed. Finally, Igor handed us pictures of himself. 'Which border crossing you go?' he said. 'I make call. You have no problems.'

We roared down the road, whooping loudly to release pent-up tension.

'Fucking hell, Charley,' I shouted over the intercom. 'I don't know what that was all about, and part of me loved it, but doesn't it feel great to get away?'

CHARLEY: About an hour later we were at the Russian border. It took us fourteen hours to enter the Ukraine and only fifteen minutes to leave. We'll never know whether that was the result of Igor's phone call, but our passports and customs documents were given only a cursory glance.

'You!' one of the guards said to me. 'You. Do this!' He revved an imaginary motorbike and lifted his hands. He wanted a wheelie. I was only too happy to oblige. I climbed on to my bike and hoicked a little wheelie on the tarmac in front of the guards' huts.

'No! Here!' the guard said, pointing through the border. I couldn't believe it. A member of one of the world's most uptight bureaucracies wanted me to wheelie across his nation's frontier. I swung the bike around, waved to the guards, and let rip. By the time I reached Russian soil, my front wheel was 3 feet in the air and I was doing 40mph. I banged the front wheel back down and looked back. One of the border guards was waving manically. Then he blew his whistle. Fuck, I thought, now you've really blown it, Charley.

Slowly I rolled towards him, expecting to be torn from my bike and dragged into a dirty office for, at best, a severe dressing down.

'Again!' he said, smiling broadly and holding up his camera. He'd missed the shot and wanted another chance to take a picture. I revved the Beamer, a guard lifted the barrier and I roared through the border once more. It doesn't get much better than this, I thought. First the night of guns and vodka with Igor; now in all likelihood I'd become the first person to execute a motocross stunt into the former USSR.

Death, war and pride

BELAYA KALITVA TO AKTOBE

2431

EWAN: By early evening we were in Belaya Kalitva and with its concrete corridors, Formica-clad doors, Titanic-era plumbing and multi-coloured bathroom tiles, the hotel was an assault on the senses, but I loved it. It felt as if we really *were* somewhere else. 'We're in Russia for God's sake, Charley,' I said. 'I'm so excited.'

Charley was exhausted and that night, over dinner, the strain of the previous few days began to show. He was very negative, cutting off Russ, David and Sergey in mid-sentence and then, as we talked about whether the journey would change our lives, he stood up. 'Fuck life changing,' he snapped. 'We're just a couple of wankers riding around the world on bikes.' Then he stormed off.

I certainly didn't feel like a wanker on a bike and I'd been so touched by the lives of the many people we had seen and met, that I felt I couldn't avoid being affected by it. Charley was just letting his tiredness get in the way, and next day, as I watched him listen to a guide telling us about the Cossacks and their history of being persecuted and exploited by the tsars and the communists, I could see that he was moved by their attempts to rekindle a community.

A young kid gave us a demonstration of Cossack riding skills, lying on his back on the horse as it galloped around an arena, making it bow and encouraging it to lift its front legs. There was an incredible affinity between the boy and the horse, and it had made a real impression on Charley. He even popped a little wheelie for the kid as we left.

We made for Volgograd, riding across a pancake-flat landscape, whipped by a harsh wind. With wide, open plains, the gusts were exhausting. They buffeted my body and thumped my head, sending my bike veering sideways. I spent half the 170 miles to Volgograd riding with my eyes half-closed.

In Volgograd, our hotel was a former haunt of senior communist party cadres, the KGB and Politburo members when they were in town. We ate early and went for a sauna across the road in a banya used by generations of Russian leaders. Sweating in the steam rooms and being beaten with oak branches was just what we needed. We got back to the hotel to discover that Claudio had passed his motorbike riding test. He was now on his way to Volgograd. It was fantastic news. Now we could take on the most demanding part of the trip with a cameraman in tow instead of having to worry about how to film it ourselves. I couldn't have been happier.

My only concern was the relationship between Charley and me. At times it felt a bit strained, our special dynamic upset when we were with the support crew.

CHARLEY: The next morning we left for Astrakhan. We passed a massive oil refinery and factories that stretched for hours along the route out of Volgograd, and then came a smooth road across a wide open landscape following the Volga down to the Caspian Sea for the rest of the day. The mood was great and remained that way even when we were stopped by the police, Ewan playing the Obi-Wan card by showing them a picture of himself in *Star Wars*. They waved us through: bliss.

The fertile plains turned into a sandy desert landscape, we spotted our first Kazakh faces and for the first time it felt as if we were really out in the cuds. 'Kazakhstan tomorrow,' I shouted to Ewan. 'The 'stan, man!' It was early evening and we were in Astrakhan, pulling up outside the hotel, where an attractive Russian woman was playing with her daughter, who immediately triggered pangs of homesickness for our daughters. A man came out and spoke to the woman.

'I heard your voice,' Ewan said, 'and I'm thinking that sounds like a Scottish accent.'

'Och aye,' the man said. 'From Kirkcaldy.'

'Never! I spent a year at drama school there. What are you doing here?'

'Working on the oil.'

'Well, it's nice to meet you. We're doing a world tour. Northern hemisphere, that is.'

We'd ridden more than 2,800 miles and bumped into someone who, as Ewan put it, came from 'jooost arooond the corner'. Maybe the world was a smaller place than it seemed after long days in the saddle.

The next morning we crossed the Russian border. We then had a five- or six-mile ride to a river in the Volga delta. On the other shore was Kazakhstan – just a short ferry ride separated Europe from Asia. On the European side there was a concrete purpose-built landing jetty; on the Asian side, nothing. The captain powered the flat-bottomed craft on to a sandy ridge, opened the gate and we rode our bikes up the riverbank.

Already it felt very different. We passed through the Kazakh frontier, a row of shabby huts, and there in front of us was a welcoming committee. Eric, our local fixer, was standing next to the mayor of the region. Two young women dressed in traditional outfits were holding trays of fermented camel's milk. It tasted fizzy, like carbonated goat's yoghurt. God, it was horrible. The formalities over, a police car accompanied us to lunch with the mayor.

'So how far is it to Almaty?' I asked. The town was our next major stop.

'More than three thousand kilometres,' said Eric. It was two-thirds the distance we had ridden so far. We were closer to Prague than we were to Almaty, the former capital and the commercial heart of the country.

'For half the route, the roads are okay,' Eric said. 'But from Atyrau to the Aral Sea they're really bad.'

We had a target of two hundred miles a day, but immediately the road turned into a rough dirt track, covered in gravel, a nightmare for motorbikes. I was petrified. According to Eric, these roads were good. They'd get much worse later. I felt overwhelmed.

'Jesus, this is gonna be absolutely exhausting.' It was Ewan. 'We're about ten minutes into Kazakhstan and I'm already knackered.'

EWAN: About fifteen miles into Kazakhstan, the road disappeared altogether and we had to bump down a slope on to a scrappy track, which we followed until the tarmac road reappeared several miles later. The landscape, however, was magnificent. An endless emptiness. We passed our first camel, standing in the middle of the road and staring at us as we passed by.

'Let's stop.' It was Claudio, wanting to film. We pulled over. While Claudio got his camera ready, Charley and I larked around.

'Here we are in deepest Kazakhstan,' Charley whispered in David Attenborough's breathy manner. 'And right behind me is a very rare camel. *Camel camelodocus.*' Plop! The camel, unfazed by our antics, dropped some shit on the road.

'I scared it shitless,' I joked. We looked around. We were surrounded by desert. Our bikes were parked side by side, the gravel road stretching into the distance. 'It's perfect,' I said. 'It says it all. Let's take a picture.' Claudio put down his video camera while Charley and I positioned ourselves in front of the bikes. We waited for a lorry to pass. Then a white Lada appeared from behind Claudio and stopped right next to him. There were two men in the front and two in the back.

Charley and a curious camel.

'*Zdravstvuite*,' we said – hello in Russian. The men smiled back. The driver opened his door, looked down at the camera and then up at Claudio. Just as I was about to launch into our spiel about going round the world on a bike, one of the guys pulled out a gun, pointed it at Charley, then at me. I could see straight down the barrel. Oh fuck, I thought, oh no. Then the guy with the gun burst out laughing. I could see two rows of gold teeth. The driver slammed the front door shut and they sped off, leaving me shaking like a leaf.

'*Jeeez . . . us.*' It was Charley, tapping his chest as if to say: that gave me a fucking heart attack.

'It was really weird,' Claudio said, laughing. He thought it was hilarious. 'He was pointing it right at you.'

'Fuck . . .' I said. 'I could see right down the barrel.'

'No you couldn't,' Charley said. 'He was pointing at me. I could see right down the barrel.'

'Don't worry about it,' Claudio said. 'He was just having a laugh.' Pragmatic as ever, for Claudio facing a loaded gun was nothing new. He'd been filming in war zones since the 1980s and had even interviewed Osama bin Laden, long before most of us had heard of him. But Charley and I were stunned, our enthusiasm for the trip ahead immediately drained.

The roads got worse. And worse. And when we thought they couldn't possibly become any more challenging, they deteriorated even more. Clouds covered the sun, the wind picked up, the temperature plummeted and I dreamed of a hot bath. Forty miles short of Atyrau we were stopped by a policeman. Massively fat with a monster-sized cap, he looked like a big cuddly bear. Harrumphing and shaking his head, he refused to let us go any further without a full police escort. With the Lada's lights flashing, siren blazing and the fat policeman bellowing through a megaphone, ordering the traffic to let us through red lights and crossroads, it wasn't quite the unannounced entrance into town we had planned, but at least we wouldn't have to search for our hotel.

I spotted a crowd ahead, gathered in a lay-by. As we approached, a bank of lights was switched on and I realised I was staring at a pack of journalists. The police car pulled in and the policeman jumped out. 'Stay here,' he instructed.

I was tired and I couldn't think of anything intelligent to say to the pestering cameras. All I wanted was a shower and food. The police car moved off, we tucked in behind it and the journalists trailed in our wake. Once at the hotel, the bun fight started again, the cameras following us into the hotel and surrounding us in the lobby as Charley, Claudio and I tried to check in. Everybody wanted to shake our hands and get an autograph from each of us. That accomplished, they left us alone. Peace and rest at last.

CHARLEY: The next morning we boarded a boat for a short cruise down the Ural to the Caspian Sea to see caviar fishermen at work. The old pleasure boat smelled wonderfully of diesel oil and the captain was a real old sea dog with a raggedy white moustache, a battered old cap and one of those bulbous noses we suspected came from drinking too much vodka. The boat ride gave us time to assess our progress so far and make plans for the journey to Almaty. One day into Kazakhstan and we were struggling to keep on schedule. We also had to face the fact that the worsening road conditions made it more likely that one of us would fall off, or that we would damage our bikes.

'Its just the amount of it that's to come that frightens me,' Ewan said. 'All of Kazakhstan could be dreadful. Then we're into Mongolia, where there are no roads, and then Siberia and the Road of Bones. I'm really concerned about how we are going to cope with it day in day out.'

EWAN: Hoping to evade a police escort, we departed early the next morning, but it was pointless. A policeman had been waiting in his car since dawn, and we rode out of Atyrau in the same manner that we'd arrived. Then we pressed on, the three of us just happy to be on the road again.

'Look at that truck!' It was Charley on the intercom. 'The last few trucks I've seen coming this way were plastered in mud. Absolutely covered in it. Don't quite know what it means, but I can't help feeling it might not be good.'

Ewan and Claudio on a fishing boat on the Caspian Sea. Claudio, our cameraman, was the unsung hero of the trip.

We got the answer a short while later when we arrived in a nondescript town. It was ankle-deep in sloppy, runny mud. 'These fucking roads,' Charley fumed. 'Jesus! If they're like this it's going to take us a very, very long time.' The mud was every biker's worst nightmare. The only way to get through it was to keep the speed up, standing on our pegs to control the balance of weight between the back wheel for traction and the front wheel for steering, but one tiny wobble and we slipped over.

A few miles later, as we rounded a bend, Claudio lost control of his bike. He went down with a crunch, the back of his bike slipping wide. He got up slowly, clutching his sides. 'I'm okay,' he said. 'That hurt, but I'm okay.'

The roads became even worse. Charley, the most experienced off-road rider, led from the front. 'Fuck, this is daunting,' Charley said. 'If this is what Siberia will be like for the entire length of the Road of Bones, then we are totally fucked.'

Our slow progress meant we would have to camp. I wanted to sleep in a tent, but Charley was less keen and our doctor, Vasiliy, had advised us against it. 'Is impossible now,' Vasiliy insisted. 'Now season for high activity of black widow spider. If you step on it, spider will bite. Even narcotic not make this pain less. Very pain.'

That was enough to tip it for Charley, who at the best of times didn't like the idea of camping. 'The season for black widows? We never thought about that . . .' But Charley had always known we'd have to camp.

7 ▶▶▶

▶ ▶ ▶ ▶

Free as an eagle

ROAD OF DEATH TO SEMEY

5703

MILES

EWAN: Next day, although it was cold and windy, the road was much smoother than anything we'd encountered so far and we made quick progress. By that evening, we were standing on a pancake-flat plain beneath a tangerine-coloured moon, our tent erected behind us and a warm supper in our bellies. We'd turned off the road and ridden a few miles across the scrub to a blue lake, the perfect spot for making camp. I wallowed in the serenity and sense of independence. It didn't matter that we hadn't had a bath or shower for a couple of days. Bad hair had never felt so good.

Even Charley had to concede it was beautiful. We sat on a small hillock, eating chocolate, watching the crimson sun slip below the horizon and talking about the day. 'What a spot,' I said. 'Surely this is better than some anonymous hotel room?'

'Yeah, it's bloody paradise,' Charley said with mock misery as we threw stones into the river and the sun disappeared. 'Actually, it's not bad at all.' And he hummed the banjo tune from *Deliverance*. 'Squeal like a pig, boy . . .'

'Yeah, it's bloody paradise
...actually, it's not bad at all.'
CHARLEY

CHARLEY: I slept like a log. It must have been the fresh air. I'd surprised myself how much I'd liked camping. I couldn't quite shake off my fear of being bitten by a black widow but I did feel much more relaxed about it.

We rode for a few hours, stopping at a building sporting a bright green KAFFE sign for some water. A stone hut in the middle of nowhere, tumbleweed and dust devils blowing across the road. As I was taking off my helmet, a green Russian jeep arrived, pulling up just inches away. Two men, both small and wearing leather baseball caps, stepped out. We smiled but they just stared back blankly at us, then walked past into the café.

'They're a bit unfriendly,' Ewan said. I felt very uneasy.

While the two men were inside the café, another pair turned up: security guards from a nearby factory. Seconds later, the unfriendly men emerged from the café, gripping two large kitchen knives in their fists. Fuck, I thought, we're going to get robbed. Then the men with the knives spotted the security guards. Quick as a flash, they hid the kitchen knives behind their backs and sauntered casually over to their jeep and drove off. It was hard to escape the feeling that we'd just avoided a potential hold-up.

But there was little time to consider what might have happened. 'Fuck, I'm exhausted,' Ewan said. 'We've only done thirty-eight miles this morning and already I feel like I've done a day's riding.' It had been a tough morning. A lot of sand and gravel. The only way to cope with it was to keep your speed up, just barrel through it and hope for the best.

Ewan was in low spirits by the time we stopped for lunch at another café. He had a tendency to impose his moods on everyone surrounding him. One minute he was up, the next he'd hit the bottom of a deep trough. I'd learned the hard way that the best thing was to accept it and wait for him to get over it. He could snap out of a bad mood as quickly as he entered it. But it was a pain in the arse.

EWAN: I was really missing my wife and my kids and with at least two hundred off-road miles to ride by the end of the day, I found it difficult to raise my spirits.

Fed up with riding at the back, I insisted on taking the lead. Suddenly I found my rhythm. I was back in the zone, reaching a decent speed on the sandy stretches, imagining I was in the Paris–Dakar rally and picking the fastest line through the potholes. The next thing I knew, I was on the ground and the sun was beating down on me. Overconfident, I'd lost control and fallen again. We ploughed on, riding an emotional and physical rollercoaster.

The long hours in the saddle gave me time to let my thoughts drift. My job had always been very important for me, but now I felt divorced from it. I had nothing lined up for when the trip was over and I felt as if I was in limbo, unsure of which step I should take next. I didn't want to give up acting, but should I spend a year working in the theatre? Or was it time to direct a film or a play? I'd always been driven more by seeking out interesting projects than thinking what would be good for my career, but maybe now was the time to take stock and decide how to move forward.

The trip was also giving me the opportunity to contemplate things that had happened to me and to lay them to rest. I was carrying a lot of emotional baggage that needed time to be worked through and left behind. I also contemplated the good things that had happened, like meeting Eve, getting married and having children. Most surprising of all was that I seemed to have no control over the thoughts; they just popped into my head as if to say 'Remember me? We go back a long way'. And if it was an uncomfortable thought, I had no choice but to sit with it and work it through. And that was a good thing.

By that evening we were riding almost entirely on soft golden sand and my legs were again shaking from standing on my pegs all day. Charley wanted to sleep in a hotel. 'I just want a bath,' he pleaded. But having failed in our ambition of reaching Aral, we camped in the desert among some old mud-hut ruins. With the birds twittering nearby and the mosquitoes buzzing around us, we scoffed our dinners hungrily, watching the sun come down on the hardest day's riding we'd ever experienced.

CHARLEY: The next day I awoke to find Manimal sleeping beside me. A mosquito bite had swollen into a massive lump stretching right across Ewan's forehead and on to the bridge of his nose, making him look like Neanderthal man. His arms were just as bad, the skin tight and sore around a string of mosquito bites. I felt sorry for him, and the roads that morning were just as awful as before. You couldn't have made them worse if you had bombed them. We had vastly overestimated the distances we would manage in Kazakhstan, but given that we'd managed more than 250 miles the previous day, I was encouraged that we'd be able to make up lost time in Mongolia.

We reached Aral around lunchtime and what was once the world's fourth largest expanse of inland water was nowhere to be seen. Since the 1960s, when the Soviet government redirected the Syr Darya and Amu Darya rivers to irrigate cotton and vegetable fields in Uzbekistan and other parts of Kazakhstan, the water level had fallen by about 50 feet and the Aral Sea had split into two much smaller lakes containing water that was now three times saltier than sea water and the once abundant stocks of sturgeon, roach, carp and other fish had died out. The only sign of its maritime heritage was a line of rusting fishing boats lying on the sand, the sea now out of sight, over the horizon.

A short distance beyond Aral, the mud ended and we were riding on tarmac for the first time in three days. We put as many miles as we could under our wheels as the temperature plummeted and at Qyzylorda, Ewan and I stood in the foyer of a hotel. We'd just made it. 'I hit the wall out there,' Ewan said. 'I couldn't ride another mile.'

We'd put nearly four hundred miles behind us and we were both physically finished and emotionally drained. After forty-eight hours of dusty roads and living in each other's pockets, I wanted a bit of privacy. More than anything I wanted a shower. I stood under the hot water for half an hour, slowly thawing out.

Ewan on the brink of complete exhaustion ...

EWAN: The sun burst into my bedroom, waking me up. It was a cool, crisp morning and soon we were back on a tarmac road, floating along at 80mph and it felt fantastic. I was in the best mood I'd been in for a week, singing in my helmet, just having a laugh. The desert gave way to more fertile plains, dotted with lines of cypress trees. We came across a little yurt, the first we'd seen, so we piled in. It was beautifully decorated with brightly coloured fabrics but a bit smelly. 'I think they let the camels sleep in here,' Charley said. We had some tea and got back on our bikes.

I put some Beatles on my iPod and rode along listening to the music. 'The Long and Winding Road' came on, and blasting out the words inside my helmet, I felt fantastic.

We stopped in the town of Turkestan to visit Kazakhstan's most important building, a turquoise-domed mausoleum to Kozha Akhmed Yasaui. It was a most beautiful, tranquil building inside and out.

After the mausoleum visit, we were promised a swift lunch with the local head of tourism, then we were given a police escort that surpassed anything we'd experienced so far. This particular police Lada never slowed below 75mph. He veered from one side to the other, barging cars out of our way – truck, motorcycle, Lada or Mercedes-Benz, it didn't matter what they were. It was nerve-racking. We later discovered the policeman had driven so aggressively because he was concerned we would arrive in Shymkent after it was dark.

Shymkent was the venue for a demonstration of goat polo, the national game. It involved two teams of four players on horseback, dressed in large hats and wearing leather boots, scrapping over the carcass of a headless goat. While folk music blared, the players grabbed the 35-kilogram carcass, hauled it up onto their horse, galloped up the field and attempted to hurl it through the opposition's goal.

It was a phenomenal spectacle, mainly because of the Kazakh's incredible horsemanship. After the match, they demonstrated a Kazakh version of kiss chase in

which a male rider chased a woman on horseback, lifting his hat every time he managed to kiss her. Then they turned around and galloped back towards us, the girl raising her hat every time she managed to whip the male rider. At the end, they asked if I would like a ride.

I was up on the horse in a flash, Charley following immediately afterwards. We galloped off down the track and at the end of the straight, I stopped and turned. 'Race you back!' I shouted, digging my heels in.

The horses were fantastic animals, hardier and faster than anything I'd ridden before. I got a head start on Charley then, slowly, a horse's head appeared beside me and we were side by side. Charley had to be in front, even if it meant he had a heart attack. We galloped on, riding closer than I had ever done before, reaching the finish line neck and neck. It was a dead heat. I looked over at Charley, a smile like a Cheshire cat on his face. A brilliant moment.

CHARLEY: We left Shymkent early the next morning on a mission to reach Almaty, 450 miles away. Riding under a clear blue sky towards the Tien Shan, a line of snow-capped mountains that stretched across the horizon separating Kazakhstan and Krygyzstan from China and forming one of the world's longest borders, the air smelled fantastic and I felt great. This was really what it was all about.

Almaty was a bustling, cosmopolitan city, thronging with Hummers and big BMW and Mercedes 4×4s. After a week in the outback of Kazakhstan, it was quite a culture shock to be riding through a comparatively wealthy city of two million people. Nearly all the roads in the centre were lined with mature trees, the buildings standing some way behind them. It gave a charming impression of driving through a thick forest, the tree-lined avenues hiding expensive designer clothes shops, glitzy nightclubs, good restaurants and high-class hotels.

The Unicef project at the Tamgaly climbing centre is an essential outlet for local teenagers.

We spent four days in Almaty, recuperating, servicing the bikes, eating well and going out late, and visiting a Unicef project, the Tamgaly climbing centre, a mountain gorge in the Tien Shan range about two hours from Almaty. With funding from British Airways, Unicef had set up a project that provided climbing lessons and facilities for 22,000 seven- to fourteen-year-olds in Kazakh schools. Social problems such as drug abuse and crime among adolescents had avalanched since the collapse of communism, but I could see from the children at the climbing competition that the climbing clubs had helped them build up confidence, adopt a healthy lifestyle and make friends. Those schools that had climbing walls installed experienced less truancy.

The next day, Ewan and I visited one of the best climbers, Akmaral Doskaraeva, a fourteen-year-old girl who lived in a shanty town on the outskirts of Almaty. Akmaral's mother, Gulbashim, and her husband had moved from the countryside to Almaty to find a job. For six months they searched for somewhere to live, not knowing if they would ever see their children again. When Gulbashim told the story, I could see in the face of Ismeral, Akmaral's seven-year-old sister, the absolute terror that still haunted her. It wasn't uncommon for parents never to return for their children, simply because they could not afford to travel back to their home village or to bring their children to join them. They lived in a tiny house. One room was a kitchen and bathroom, the other was the living room and bedroom. Both were smaller than the bathroom in my Almaty hotel suite.

On the morning of 12 May, when we rode out of Almaty bound for the Charyn Canyon, I looked at the picture of my daughters taped to the inside of my windscreen. I'd been away from them for only four weeks, yet I missed them terribly. I couldn't imagine what it would be like to walk away from your children in search of a better life, not knowing for sure whether you would ever see them again . . .

We rode past disused checkpoints that twenty years earlier had controlled access to the highly sensitive Soviet-Sino border. Such a vast frontier was thought to be almost uncontrollable, prompting jokes in the Soviet era that the Chinese had instructed their troops to move only in small units of ten thousand soldiers or less.

Then, suddenly, there it was in front of us. The Valley of the Castles. Formed by the Charyn River, which flowed rapidly down from the snow-capped peaks of the Tien Shan, the canyon sank more than 300 metres beneath the desert plain. With ambitions of camping at the bottom of the canyon, amidst the red weathered rock formations, we followed a track that led downwards. Big mistake. Several miles on it ended abruptly with a sudden vertical drop to the canyon floor. We had no choice but to turn back. But getting our bikes back up the steep, rutted track was impossible. It took us three hours to unload our bikes, cart all our luggage, piece by piece, up the narrow track, and then ride up the

Ewan at the Singing Dunes in Kazakhstan.

path. It gave me a new respect for the BMW, carrying all that weight and us in comfort for long distances every day. We learnt a valuable lesson: don't go down a track if you don't have to!

Having forgotten to seal my inflatable mattress properly, I woke in the middle of the night with nothing between me and the hard, stony ground. Inside my bivvy bag, only a mosquito net separated me from the night sky. I could see millions of stars. The Milky Way, which I had never seen so clearly before, stretched across the sky like a smeary band of fairy lights and I had an overriding feeling of wanting this journey to go on for ever. I just wanted more and more . . .

The next day was just as good. Warm air blew through our jackets as we made our way north to the Russian border, riding through a golden desert flanked to the east by the four-thousand-metre peaks of the Tien Shan. By dusk we were riding along a dusty track towards the singing dunes, Ewan and Claudio ahead of me, silhouetted in the clouds of dust, the setting sun throwing long shadows ahead of us.

Early the next morning, we pushed on towards Russia. We had several long days' riding ahead of us if we were going to cross the border by the end of the week. Still behind schedule, we were relying on making up lost mileage in Mongolia.

EWAN: We arrived at Ayaköz at ten o'clock, long after the sun had set. Claudio had hit a large pothole full pelt in the darkness, denting his front wheel rim, but we had no time to stop and worry about it. Desperate for a bed and a shower, we stupidly let our good old friends the rozzers take the lead. 'Follow us,' they said and we were too tired to argue. They led us to the town square, where a stage had been erected and some entertainment was laid on. Once again, we were caught in the hospitality dilemma. The extraordinary effort to which people went was incredibly flattering and kind, but we were dog-tired at the end of a long ride. It was our last night in Kazakhstan and it would have been churlish to refuse, so we watched the entertainment. A small crowd turned up and we ended up signing autographs and having our pictures taken with them.

We eventually ended up in a house that we believed belonged to the local Governor where a meal had been laid on for us. The table was laden with the kind of food we'd been eating all the way through Kazakhstan: shashlik, mutton stew, caviar, smoked fish, lots of salads and a mountain of bread rolls. Just as I was thinking that we were about to get through Kazakhstan without ever having to eat sheep's head, a door swung open and a woman carrying a large platter walked in. The head had been boiled, leaving a thin layer of greyish mushy flesh on it that looked like overcooked fat. I didn't know what to do so I proposed a toast.

'It's our last night in Kazakhstan and it's a night we certainly won't forget,' I said, raising my glass of water. 'Thank you very much for your hospitality and for allowing us to meet you and stay in your home.' The Governor offered a toast in Kazakh, downed his glass of vodka and then, turning to me, offered some of the sheep's head.

I was intrigued by the strange delicacy, but Charley looked worried. 'I want to see them eat it first to make sure that they're not making a joke of it,' he said.

'It's like . . .' I said, slipping a sliver of the greasy meat into my mouth. 'Actually, it's fine.'

'You're making lots of noise chewing it. You sure it's okay?'

Our hosts were ripping the sheep's head apart. Everything came off it, even the insides of the ears. Charley smiled and nodded politely, but wouldn't eat it. Fortunately, our hosts weren't offended. They thought it was amusing rather than rude.

Eventually we got the sleep we needed and the next day, we rode, via a gold mine that we visited in the morning, to Semey, close to the Russian border.

As we pushed on, I realised I didn't have a care in the world. I was drifting down a hill, marvelling at the sight of the hills and fields in front of me bathed in a beautiful golden light from the setting sun, the air fresh and heavy with the smells of the countryside, and I realised it was a perfect moment. I'd stopped worrying about the schedule; I was no longer worried about when or where we would have lunch and I'd managed to flush out my concerns about bigger issues, such as my future. For the first time in a long, long while, nothing was troubling me.

We were covering huge distances. Four hundred and seventy miles that day. Another three hundred miles ahead of us the next day. And as we followed the road, I came to feel that I belonged on that big motorcycle, rolling around the world. It didn't matter where exactly we were headed. We'd get there. We'd find somewhere to stay. Something or somebody would turn up. And if they didn't, we'd camp. It was that simple. At last I was living for each day, free as the eagles that lined the roadside, and I had the land of caviar, oil and gold to thank for that.

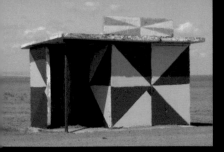

Russ started taking pictures of bus shelters in the Ukraine. The shelters became more elaborate as the trip went on and seemed to reflect the change in culture as we moved east.

8 ▶ ▶ ▶

Little Red Devil

BARNAUL TO ULAANGOM

6657

MILES

EWAN: And so we rode into Russia. Everything immediately looked different. The landscape, the people, the houses, the roads, the fields had all changed. How did it know to do that? How did everything this side of the border know it was meant to look Russian, and how did everything a few miles before know it had to look Kazakh? I was pondering this when Claudio came to a screeching halt. We all pulled over.

'So what's happening, Claudio?' I said.

'I nearly had a head-on crash,' he said. 'That was nearly it for me. I was nodding off. These roads are too easy.'

It was baking hot, and we had all stripped down to our vests. 'Funny that,' I said. 'I was just thinking about how much smoother the roads are in Russia.'

'Yeah, I was just thinking how it looks a bit like Mongolia, actually,' Charley said.

'How do you know it looks like Mongolia?' I said. 'We haven't been there yet. And anyway, it doesn't.'

'Well, it's a bit like Kazakhstan.'

'No. It doesn't look anything like Kazakhstan. It's amazing how different it looks from Kazakhstan.'

'Well . . . yeah . . . it's greener, but it's as flat.'

'It's completely different.'

'It's a different flat then,' Charley said. 'But it's still flat.'

I turned to Claudio. 'How are you feeling?'

'The roads are flatter,' Claudio said. 'No potholes.'

'You're not happy? You want potholes?'

'Yeah, because I had to concentrate,' Claudio said. 'I need a focus in life.'

Standing bare-chested at the side of the road, Charley was playing with his stomach. The only difference he would concede between Kazakhstan and Russia was the frequency at which his pot vibrated. 'This was Kazakhstan.' Charley shook his stomach violently. 'This is Russia.' Charley said, thrumming his belly gently. 'And this will be America.' No movement at all.

By late afternoon we were in Barnaul, a crazy place with the feel of a turn-of-the-century gold rush town. We showered and set off for a restaurant called 'Rock and Roll' in the hope of a wild night. Reunited with the support crew for the first time in a week, we ate a Mexican meal under the fairy lights of a restaurant terrace, told stories and had a great night. 'The cuds serve their purpose,' Charley said, 'and that's okay, but this has just made me realise how much I love cities.'

Unfortunately for Charley, we were straight back into the cuds the next day. We rode higher into the Altai Mountains, the twisty road climbing through thick forests and lush fields, and winding along meandering streams through mountain valleys carpeted with pink-purple heather. It was the best day's riding I'd ever had. It was staggeringly beautiful. Like the previous day, it was stiflingly hot. Spotting a mountain stream, we stopped, stripped off and went skinny-dipping.

'Aaaagh! Where has my penis gone?' I screamed as I stepped into the river and my body recoiled at the cold.

Claudio strode into the river, wincing slightly. 'The feet is the worst,' he said. 'Maybe it's because they get hottest in the boots.' Stepping gingerly across the stones, Charley suddenly ducked under the water and shot back up, yelling at the cold.

'This is so liberating!' I screamed, running naked along the riverbank back to my bike. 'Three nude men in the countryside. We should have some drums and bows and arrows.'

We were three and a half days behind but it didn't matter any more. I no longer felt like a tourist or a traveller. The journey had become my life.

By late afternoon we stopped to camp beside another river. We contacted the support crew via the satellite phone and arranged to camp with them for the first time. While the others collected a massive pile of firewood and made a supper of tuna and sweetcorn pasta, I got my fishing rod out. I cast a few lines, but caught nothing. Then we ate together, sitting around the huge campfire, gazing into the flames, telling ghost stories and chatting until one in the morning, taking turns to sing songs beneath the starry sky. It was a great night. We'd gone through a lot together, and Dave, Russ, Jim, Vasiliy and Sergey now felt like the best of old friends.

The riding was beautiful next day, but by the time we reached the border, I was desperate for sleep and crumpled into a heap on the concrete floor, leaving Charley and Claudio to deal with the guards.

Two hours later, we were in no-man's-land. Behind us, the Russian border, all brand new gleaming concrete and steel buildings. As we rode down a hill towards a string of shabby wooden huts that looked as if they hadn't been painted for fifty years, the tarmac ran out beneath our wheels and the gravel began. We'd got special permission to enter Mongolia from the west, and make our way to Ulaanbaatar, in the east of the country, along a route rarely travelled by tourists. The formalities quickly dealt with, we rode into Mongolia, turned a corner and ran straight into a herd of yaks. We pulled into a clearing, where our local fixer, Karina, had been waiting for four days. She was very excited and tied blue ribbons to our bikes, a Mongolian shaman tradition used to bestow good luck

on babies and vehicles. As soon as we'd had a cup of tea we whipped off, telling the support crew we'd meet them at White Lake in five or six days.

Within minutes, Charley was on the radio. 'Fucking hell, look at these roads,' he said. 'This is like going back to the fucking Stone Age. What have we let ourselves in for?' The roads were no more than tracks. As we rode in parallel across sludge-coloured plains, an immense sky threw shadows in a million shades of brown across the rolling hills and mountains and five or six tracks cut across the steppe, making it difficult to judge which one went where. Our target of one hundred miles a day would test us and it would test the bikes.

Crawling along at about 20mph, we came to our first Mongolian town. 'Talk about poverty,' Charley said.

The buildings were crumbling ruins. A man and a child appeared. Both of them looked terrible, the child filthy and barefoot with a snotty nose and sores on his arms and face. 'Oh my God,' I said, shocked.

We rode on until we came to a patch of greener ground beside a river. It was past nine o'clock and a storm was brewing, so we decided to camp. As we settled down to cook our dinner I looked up and saw a dark figure on horseback, silhouetted against a triangle of stormy sky between two mountains. A young kid, no more than fourteen, stopped about 50 feet away, and watched us warily.

'He's not coming any closer,' Charley said.

'Maybe we should approach him,' I said.

We walked up to the kid. The horse was small, a chestnut with a bushy black forelock and a white star on its snubby nose. I stroked it. 'Hello. Nice horse,' I said. The kid stared back. He had dark, suspicious eyes. We shook his hand in turn. He watched for a while, then turned his horse.

'Well . . . bye then,' I said. The kid cantered off, giving us the biggest beaming smile, all white teeth, leaving us to ponder on our first contact with the locals.

CHARLEY: We slept late, but it was good to get a proper night's sleep. Setting off with the intention of reaching Ulaangom, a market town about 130 miles east, we rode across a landscape built for giants. It was baking hot and, with no vegetation in sight, the ground and surrounding mountains glistened like gold. The sheer beauty of it took my breath away. We followed the track into a gorge that led to Bohomoron, a small town, but without signposts or proper roads it was impossible to work out which track to follow out of it. We rode back to a petrol station. Within minutes, we were surrounded by crowds of people wanting to look at our bikes. They were incredibly friendly but no help with directions. Then an old boy in a suit turned up, riding pillion on someone else's motorbike.

'Ulaangom?' I said, pointing to a map.

He shook his head and wiggled his hand to indicate a river. Then, pointing at my bike, he grabbed my map and, with his finger, sketched out a route around a large lake shown on the map.

'I think he's saying the river's too high and we have to go round Lake Achit to get to the other side of it,' I told Ewan. 'Must be about a hundred-and-fifty-mile detour.'

The man got back on the motorbike and with his friend led us a few miles out of town, where they stopped and pointed ahead, indicating that we had to follow the track around a large mountain in the distance. The main roads, which were shown as thick red lines on the map, were only dirt tracks at best. But this route was quite likely to disappear altogether at some point, leaving us stranded in the middle of Mongolia. The only thing we could do was trust our GPS navigation equipment, without which we would have been completely buggered.

Lo and behold, the track did soon disappear, leaving us to ride across wide open plains of stone and gravel and mud. Towards the end of the day, we passed through Hotgor, a mining town in which we had hoped to find a bed. But as the locals all appeared to be extremely drunk, we kept going, eventually pitching a camp on a dry riverbed.

The day had been soul-destroying. The detour around the lake meant we'd made no progress further east. 'It's like wanting to cross Leicester Square and having to go via Wales,' Ewan said.

Many Mongolian families still live
a nomadic life in gers (also known as
yurts in other parts of the world).

EWAN: Packing our bags the next morning, we discovered the luggage frame on Claudio's
bike had cracked on the left side. It was the first serious damage to any of the three BMWs.
We rode back into Hotgor to stock up on water from a tanker, dropping a couple of
purification tablets into it, and then began the first of three long climbs over mountain
passes, determined to make Ulaangom that evening.

At the top of the first pass, we came across a nomad on horseback with three camels
and a couple of dogs. He was a stunning man, fine-featured and handsome, in the
traditional garb of pointed leather herdsman's boots, a Mongolian hat and several layers
of heavy woollen clothing. He rode over slowly, climbed down from his horse and stood
at a distance, watching us. It appeared to be the Mongolian way, just taking your time to
suss out strangers. Slowly he walked over and we shook hands. He circled around the
bikes, looking them over and talking softly in a beautiful lilting voice. As we chatted, not
really understanding each other but still managing to communicate, I had an idea.

That evening we were invited into the ger by the nomads. Ornate carpets covered the bare ground; tapestries and intricately patterned fabrics lined the walls.

'Would you like to eat nuts?' our Mongolian fixer asked.

'What do you mean nuts?' Russ demanded.

'Bollocks,' Ewan said. 'Bull's testicles. I saw them castrating some animals behind the ger only an hour or so ago.'

'Noooo,' Russ said. 'No, no.'

The Mongolian woman lifted the lid on the bubbling pot. Inside was a brown liquid with a white foamy scum and what looked like lumps of gristle floating in it. She spooned

the liquid with a ladle and let the lumps plop back into the cauldron. It was unmistakable. They were testicles. Lamb's, bull's and goat's testicles. A feast for Mongolians, but a nightmare for us. Ewan was nervously stroking his beard and I had broken out in a sweat.

'Well, go on,' Russ said to me. 'You come from a farming background.'

'Why don't you do it?' I asked. Russ had turned pale.

'Just cheese, bread and tea for me. Simple tastes,' Russ said. 'Go on. Have a bull's nut.'

The woman ladled out testicles for each of us and handed us bowls to put on the little Formica-topped tables in front of us . . .

'Oh my Lord,' Russ said, looking wide-eyed at his portion.

► ► ►

Snow in my ger

BARUUNTURUUN TO CHITA

6760

MILES

EWAN: For half an hour we waited before David called back.

'Hey, yes, everyone's okay . . . Jesus Christ, it's a mess . . . The car was on its fucking roof. But they're okay . . . shaken obviously, but okay.'

David explained what had happened. One of the rear tyres had blown as Russ was driving up a bank. The back of the truck had swung around and it had overturned twice before coming to rest on its roof. David, Jim and our Mongolian fixers had pulled Russ and Vasiliy, who had hurt his back badly, out of the pick-up.

And then David let the shock show: 'I mean . . . fuck. You know? Fucking . . . I could see the whole thing happening.' He took a deep breath. 'So why did you call me in the first place, Ewan?' Our problems seemed so trivial now, but I still needed to consult David on our proposal.

'Russ and I won't take any part in your decision. It's your call,' David said. 'But let me just say this: this could be something you regret for the rest of your lives . . . When we scheduled the trip we didn't speak to anybody who'd ridden across Mongolia on a motorcycle. And would putting an extra week on the schedule be the end of the world?'

As David was speaking, I thought back to the previous evening, when I had stood in the rain, watching the sons of the wonderful nomad family bringing in the herd. There were about four hundred beasts – goats, sheep, cows and yaks. Watching these young lads work, silhouetted against the darkening sky, riding across a huge, open, twilit plain was the most beautiful sight. Shapes from centuries ago: men on horseback, herding animals in silence, their outlines softened by the rain. It was beautiful and it moved me.

By the time David had finished speaking, I was completely turned around. I told Charley and he took it well.

'Let's adjust our route,' he said.

Right: Russ and Vasiliy were both in this support vehicle when it crashed – rolling over twice. Amazingly, no one was seriously hurt.

CHARLEY: Inevitably, we fell over again. And, equally inevitably, the Red Devil broke down again. This time a different set of Mongolians came to our rescue. Two wore western clothes. The third, a ninety-seven-year-old in a purple silk tunic and trousers, with a pink scarf wrapped around his head, sat to the side, smoking a long wooden pipe with a metal bowl and watching the other two. When it was finished, the old boy offered us all a snort of his snuff. In return, we gave him some Kendal Mint Cake and some of our whisky miniatures.

I'd got used to the idea of not heading for Russia. It was only three or four months out of my life. Just suck it up and enjoy it, I told myself, don't pussy around. And while I was thinking about this, Baruunturuun appeared ahead. The town at last.

Baruunturuun was a sizable town, full of vibrant people. A middle-aged clean-cut Mongolian man approached us. He spoke English, said he lived in Ulaanbaatar, and he went through the route with me. The bad news was that we had six hundred miles of the same kind of tracks ahead of us but the route was very scenic. The good news was that the last four hundred miles to UB were tarmac.

Then the support team turned up, and Russ's pick-up truck, nicknamed the Animal, trundled into town looking as if it had been through a crusher. The windscreen was missing and David was wearing ski goggles to drive it. 'We didn't have a good day,' he said.

They'd used a rope and pulley to drag the Animal upright then a hydraulic jack to lift the dented roof so that they could shut the driver's door. The tailgate was wide open, pointing at the sky. It could no longer be closed.

The next day started well. We took a track up into the mountains and had the best morning's trail riding we'd ever experienced. With snowcaps in the distance, we passed gers and nomads riding with their camels, yaks, horses, sheep and goats. There were rivers running through pine forests and green lush pastures. Ewan was on a high, but I couldn't shake off my fear that the easy conditions wouldn't last and that we'd get lost. And I was right: we descended into a valley, it had been raining and the ground just turned to bog. In less than an hour I couldn't see any tyre tracks anywhere.

We pushed on, the tracks becoming much more boggy, and then we came to our first really wide river. We crossed it with little difficulty, kept going and then crossed it again as the track and the river wove around and across each other.

On our third crossing there was a ger on the bank and a couple of herdsmen nearby. Ewan went first. He got as far as halfway, then stopped. He'd hit a rock. I couldn't put my bike down because there was nowhere to put it safely on its stand, so Ewan was stuck. I shouted at the herdsmen. They saw what was happening and steamed in to help. Then it was my turn. I entered the river with my stomach in my mouth, but made it across. Claudio, of course, just scooted through without a care in the world.

We rode on for another two miles, until the road faded. I decided we ought to turn back, but it meant that we had to cross back over the river again. This time I decided to park up and walk behind Ewan's bike, holding the back as he rode through the water. But while I was finding somewhere safe to leave my bike, Ewan lost control of his, dropping it so that it was lying almost upside down, smashing one of the fog lamps and scratching the petrol tank.

Again, the herdsmen helped us get the bikes across the river and we set off on a different track. The conditions became increasingly boggy and we all fell a number of times. Our stamina was flagging and then it started to rain very hard and I got really worried. If we don't get a move on, I thought, we'll get stuck in this valley. We'll never get out.

And then it started to snow.

I couldn't take it any more. Stuck in a bog, I caught my bike before it fell, but it was too heavy: I was unable to pull it upright on my own. Ewan ran over to help me lift it, then returned to his bike and moved off gingerly, entering a puddle and immediately falling over himself. Claudio then ran to Ewan's aid and in pushing him out was drenched in mud.

'Oh, Claudio, fucking hell. I'm sorry, mate,' Ewan said. 'Whatever happened to just a bit of tarmac, you know, just a little bit of asphalt? Whatever happened to dry clothes? Whatever happened to being able to sit on a motorbike without falling off it? And why is it that you've hardly fallen off at all?'

It was too much. I just burst into tears in my helmet. It had taken us two hours to ride six miles. It was a nightmare and all I could think was that we still had Siberia ahead of us. We'd covered less than thirty-five miles that day, but, with even darker clouds approaching, I thought there was nothing for it but to head for a copse of trees to camp.

As we climbed off our bikes, the rain stopped for a short while and Claudio spoke up. 'Let's get out of this valley,' he said. 'If it rains tonight we'll be stuck here for days.'

Claudio was right. We had no choice but to press on. But it became a lot worse.

The tracks became less and less distinct, merging into one big squirming mess, and the grass became more and more sodden and slippery. Eventually we spotted some telegraph poles and used them to navigate. The road became slightly better and we climbed a long hill. When we got to the top, everything changed. It was if someone had drawn a line across the landscape. Behind us, a mud bath. Ahead, rocky desert.

The track now dry, we rode another twenty miles to Ondorhangay. As we entered the town, I spotted a white car passing through very carefully, which I took to be a good sign. We followed it and as we were reaching the edge of the little town I raced over to the car, stopped it and asked the lady who was driving it how to get to Songino, our next destination. She said to follow her and took us to a track by the river that we'd crossed to get into the town. We rode through the river and then followed her directions on to the smoothest piece of road we'd yet seen in Mongolia. We glided along at 40mph. It was fantastic. Ewan was very wet and very cold, so we decided to continue for another forty-five minutes to let his clothes dry. Then we stopped and camped.

I was euphoric. We'd survived the mud, rivers and bogs. We'd done it. It was a fantastic achievement. 'At least it's good practice for Siberia,' I said. 'Surely it can't be any worse than this?'

The ride the next day to Nomrog was fantastic. Running through the desert, the track was as smooth as glass. The sun was shining, it was windy, we didn't make too many mistakes and the scenery was just fantastic. By early afternoon we'd put nearly one hundred miles under our wheels.

We had a very long journey the next day via Tosontsengel, where we had a fantastic lunch, to White Lake. In the late afternoon, we came screaming down a long pass towards a large bridge. There, standing beside the bridge, was the support team. It was great to see them. It meant we'd all got through the toughest part of the journey, a fantastic achievement.

I'd come to love Mongolia. It had been hell at times, but some part of me had actually relished the misery. I'd enjoyed meeting people along the road and I'd been blown away by the helpfulness of complete strangers. I hadn't felt this happy for a long time: probably not since I'd been at home, in the arms of my family.

The whole crew met up the night after the crash.
It was such a relief to see everyone safe and well.

EWAN: Once we got to White Lake I spent a whole day lying in a ger, too tired even to unpack. Lying on the bed, I felt physically sick with the accumulated exhaustion of two weeks' riding in very difficult conditions. I felt extraordinarily homesick, or more pertinently, family-sick. The next morning I woke up to see snowflakes falling. All the mountains wore a dusting of snow and we were planning to cross several mountain passes. Christ, what will they throw at us next, I thought.

It was a beautiful ride up the hill behind the camp, past an extinct volcano, and the roads were fantastic. Everyone's spirits were soaring as we crossed some stupendous mountain passes and swept through some stunning gorges. We stopped for lunch at a little café in Tsetserleg run by two English people. It was bizarre, to say the least, to find what looked just like an English café, with English music, burgers, all-day breakfasts and even Sunday roasts, in the middle of the Mongolian desert.

We rode on, Claudio's bike breaking down with monotonous regularity, until I had a spill. About ten minutes later, Claudio came off, going very fast. He landed heavily on his ribs and was in quite a lot of pain.

'How are your ribs, Claudio?' Charley asked. 'Not that I really care . . .'

'They're okay,' Claudio said, but we could tell from the way he was standing that he was in a lot of pain. Charley let Claudio drive his bike and rode the Red Devil the last few miles to the ger camp. A few hundred yards from the camp, the dirt track ran out and the tarmac began. That was it. No more ruts, mud and dust. Asphalt all the way to Ulaanbaatar and past the capital to the Russian border. Charley hopped off the Red Devil and threw himself on the ground.

'Aaah,' he sighed. 'Such beautiful tarmac. Look how smooth it is. And it's warm and hard.'

'And it's Mongolia . . . ,' I said.

'Mwah!' Charley was kissing the road. 'Oh, it's so nice.'

'Charley,' I said. 'C'mon. We're just about there, c'mon!'

'I might just chill out here for half an hour,' Charley said. 'Just enjoy the tarmac.'

'I'll see you over there,' I said, pointing at the ger camp.

'Oh, that's great,' Charley said sarcastically. 'We go together through the whole of Mongolia and he fucks off now. You know? That's it. Our relationship is over. It's *over*!'

But there was some truth behind Charley's joke. After more than seven weeks constantly in each other's company, we'd had enough. We were going to ditch the tent we'd shared since Kazakhstan and get two one-man tents in Ulaanbaatar. We'd come to realise we couldn't be in each other's hair twenty-four hours a day. It was too much.

In Ulaanbaatar we found Ted Simon waiting in the foyer of our hotel. We couldn't have hoped for a better greeting. Ted, who had taken four and a half years to ride round the world on a motorbike before writing up his experience in *Jupiter's Travels*, was one of the reasons I now found myself in Mongolia. 'If I need anyone to blame for going round the world,' I said, 'Ted, you're the man.' It was great to hang out with him and just compare experiences on the road. Now seventy-three, he'd recently returned from undertaking the same journey a second time. He'd followed the same route, but found much of the world had changed for the worse since his first circumnavigation.

We spent three days with Ted. Claudio's BMW was repaired, so Ted was given the little Red Devil, cheerfully claiming to love every minute he spent on it with us riding around the city and into the nearby countryside. He also came along to the centrepiece of our stopover in Ulaanbaatar, a Unicef-organised visit to meet some street children.

The city was an ugly blot on Mongolia's stunning landscape with a filthy power station near its centre expelling dirty smoke into the atmosphere and pumping hot water along city streets through massive asbestos-clad pipes. Since Mongolia shook off its Soviet satellite status in the 1990s the number of street children had mushroomed. Unemployment had soared, welfare services declined and the gap between rich and poor widened. Beneath the bustling streets a community of children lived in a rabbit's warren of chambers built around the hot-water pipes. Some were as young as two. We met a group of about ten boys in a busy street in a commercial district and then climbed with them through a manhole into the dusty, stifling maintenance pit they called home. It was distressing to see children living in such conditions. They were tough and cocky, but, despite all they had seen and experienced, they were still very much young children. I wanted to throw my arms around all of them.

Previous page: We arrive in Ulaanbaatar.

Left: In Ulaanbaatar scores of orphans live under the streets in appalling conditions. We visited some of the children and a nearby orphanage with Unicef.

A visit to a government centre for
street children. The suffering
we saw there affected us deeply.

195

The next day we went to a government centre that provided shelter and food for the street children. There were about forty children at the centre, most of them very young, including a two-year-old girl who had been living on the streets with her four-year-old brother. A four-year-old girl was lying on the floor with her head against the wall. Her legs were withered and weak and she was trembling. It broke my heart to see her in such distress, so in need of love and attention, but so alone. I spent quite a lot of time with her, stroking her hair, touching her face and playing peek-a-boo with her. And then we had to leave. I hugged as many of them as I could, said goodbye and got into a car.

I was haunted by what I'd seen. We were planning to move on to Ulan Ude the next day, but that wee girl would still be there, so obviously ill yet not getting the care she so clearly needed. I couldn't get my head around the fact that children as young and as vulnerable as my wee daughter Esther had been abandoned and were forced to cope on their own. That unfortunate little girl had made a deeper impression on me than anything or anyone I'd seen so far on the trip. Maybe she was the mysterious woman the fortune-teller in Prague had predicted would have a profound influence upon me. We found out how much it would cost to get proper medical treatment for her and left the money with the centre. But even if this little girl received better care, there would be another child and then another to take her place. I vowed then and there to make working with Unicef something I'd do for the rest of my life . . .

We set off the next day for Ulan Ude, across the border in Russia, meeting the support crew at the frontier. I had very mixed emotions as we slipped effortlessly through the border controls. Riding across Mongolia had been incredibly demanding, but it had offered everything I'd been looking for on the trip, a pastoral paradise full of curious, open-hearted people who welcomed me into their homes because I was a passing traveller, not because I was Obi-Wan Kenobi on a bike.

CHARLEY: We had lunch in a café, which to Ewan's delight and my great surprise sold cans of Irn-Bru made in Scotland, and set off, arriving in Ulan Ude late at night. The next day we had a look around. After the tranquillity of Mongolia, it seemed a particularly busy city. Music and announcements were piped out of loudspeakers that lined dusty squares full of people sipping dark beer from plastic beakers sold out of the backs of carts. There were trams, trolley buses and stalls selling cheap sunglasses on the streets.

'We've got to think about the next section in little chunks,' Ewan said. 'The thought of riding from here to Magadan is just too much to get my head around.'

We were faced with a choice. The road from Chita to Tynda, six hundred miles further north, was – depending on who we consulted – non-existent, an old gravel track, a recently

refurbished high-quality gravel track, the base layer of a proper road and a pristine stretch of tarmac. We could either chance the road or, like every other round-the-world motorcyclist who had followed a similar route, take the train.

The next day we left the support team in Ulan Ude and rode out to Lake Baikal, the oldest freshwater lake on the planet. It held one-fifth of the world's fresh water, and we had high expectations of what we had been told was one of the most spectacular lakes on earth. It was a big disappointment – flat, marshy and uninspiring, hardly the mountain-lined beauty spot we'd been promised. We slept that night in a derelict lake-shore hut, then pressed on to Chita. Stopping for lunch, we met a truck driver who advised us to take the train from Chita to Tynda. He said we could do the Road of Bones in six days.

Our minds were made up. If we could take the train, we would. We were still reeling with exhaustion from our trek across Mongolia. Maybe a train ride would be a safer option than six hundred miles or more on a dusty gravel road.

By midday the next day we were standing in front of the impressive art nouveau frontage of Chita's main railway station. While Ewan and Claudio set off in search of tickets, I waited outside, surrounded by a crowd of winos and drug addicts, all asking questions in Russian.

'How many litres?'

'How fast does it go?'

Struggling to explain to the crowd that I didn't speak enough Russian to answer their questions, I spotted a young guy trying to get my attention. He was tall and young, with a trendy haircut and a pretty girlfriend. 'What are you doing here?' he said. 'I'm studying English in college.'

'Boy, am I pleased to meet you,' I said. 'Go into the ticket office and you'll see a guy with a shaved head, and another guy dressed in a T-shirt and trousers like mine, trying to buy a ticket. Can you give them a hand?'

And off he went, leaving me with the drunks for a very, very long time.

10 ▶ ▶ ▶

The road to Tynda was a succession of very long and extremely dusty straights. We rolled past Tynda and decided to camp; but there was nowhere to stop. Open-cast gravel mines lined both sides of the road. We continued riding, not spotting anywhere suitable until it was almost dark, when we turned off the road and crossed a riverbed. Behind me I could see Ewan getting stuck in the deep sand. Claudio and I got off our bikes and helped Ewan free his. Then we stood back and looked at his bike. His panniers were twisted and his back wheel appeared to have been knocked out of alignment.

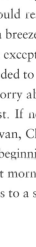

'Oh, fuck,' Ewan said. 'The luggage frame has snapped in the same place as Claudio's did.'

'I think mine's gone too,' I said. We examined our bikes. Mine had a crack on one side; Ewan's had a crack on the left and a breakage on the right.

'Oh, God.' It was Claudio. 'Ewan, look under your seat.' One of the two main bars that supported the entire back end of the bike had snapped. A disaster. Without the big, fat main bars intact, Ewan would soon have nothing to sit on.

'There's nothing for it,' I said. 'We'll have to go back to Tynda.'

We removed the panniers from Ewan's bike and patched over the breakages with tyre levers and cable ties. The next morning, we ferried his luggage piece by piece to the road, a fifteen-minute walk away.

With our top boxes and panniers in a line beside us, we sat by the side of the road hoping someone would stop and help us. Eventually, an articulated dumper truck stopped and the check-shirted driver, fag in mouth, stepped out. We explained our predicament. He nodded and pointed to the back of the truck. We threw our luggage into the dumpster, got on our bikes and followed the truck into Tynda, where a bare-chested welder and his silent assistant worked on the bikes for three hours, joining the broken frame sections. The guy was a genius and did a beautiful job, adding carefully shaped braces to the weakest points of the bikes' frames. Afterwards, we found a hotel and stripped our luggage of all the unnecessary fripperies. Weeded of all but the bare necessities, we were about 40 crucial kilograms lighter.

It took us three days to ride the eight hundred miles from Tynda to Yakutsk along dusty roads heavy with truck traffic. Day by day, our skins became darker. At first I thought I was picking up a good tan, but it was just layer upon layer of ingrained dirt.

The long journey to Yakutsk gave us plenty of opportunities to quiz truck drivers about the Road of Bones from Yakutsk to Magadan. Along the way, we accumulated so much conflicting information that we could read it any way we wanted: either the whole road was impassable or it would all be a breeze, depending on which advice we chose to believe.

We didn't do much in Yakutsk except rest and prepare our bikes and worry about the journey ahead. We desperately needed to catch up on sleep, but I spent most nights tossing and turning, unable to sleep for worry about the Road of Bones. On the last morning, we discussed our plans over breakfast. If necessary, we'd hire a truck to carry the support vehicles through the rivers, but Ewan, Claudio and I would try to ride the entire Road of Bones on our bikes. 'This is the beginning of the end of the journey,' Ewan said as we swung our legs over our bikes that morning. 'Or maybe it's the end of the beginning.'

We rode for about twenty miles to a shanty village, where we caught a ferry across the

Lena River. Meandering by inlets, the river was several miles wide at this point and as flat and still as a mirror.

The next day and a half was spent riding through the wetlands, via Matta and Chamnayy, to the next ferry. The riding was much easier than it had been in Mongolia, mainly because the bikes were so much lighter after we had dumped so much of our equipment in Yakutsk. We made quick and easy progress, eventually arriving at an empty ferry whose captain wanted $2500 to take us on a twelve-hour trip up the river.

In the town of Tomtor.

By the time we'd got off the phone to his boss, the fare had gone down to $900 and we were on the long, narrow barge. We boiled up some camping rations and ate them as the boat drifted through the twilight. After dinner, I sat on the edge of the landing ramp, one leg dangling over the side while I spoke to my wife on the satellite phone and watched the river slip past. The water was as flat as glass, the air completely still and again I had that feeling of not being at all concerned if things didn't go to plan. If only I could remain so positive when things were going against us.

This bridge was first brought to our attention at www.millennium-ride.com. Tragically, the biker who had crossed it as part of his round-the-world trip, Simon Milward, died in March 2005 before completing his journey.

We left the boat the next morning and immediately came upon the deepest gravel we'd ever experienced. The stones were about three inches across, several feet deep and a nightmare to ride on. The road had a life of its own, shifting beneath the wheels as we rode across it. It was terrifying. 'If it's going to be like this for the rest of the way, we're fucked,' I said to Ewan. It continued for mile after mile, graduating to smaller stones a few miles past Khandyga and then disappearing altogether to be replaced by hard-packed road the next day. Once we hit those hard-packed roads we screamed along at 60mph, riding through stunning countryside in monochrome: black mountains with white snowcaps, grey dirt beneath the wheels and dark rocks lining the road. And then we came to the first big river. The water was about 6 metres deep, with a ferocious current. There was a bridge nearby, but two-thirds of the way across, it had collapsed. A wooden ladder spanned the 30-foot gap between the two sections, so it was possible to cross on foot, but a bike crossing was out of the question.

We had no choice but to set up camp and wait until the river fell or a truck on which we could hitch a ride came along. I crossed the river in search of help. The town on the other side was a shithole. It was one of the former gulag concentration camps that had housed the political prisoners Stalin's regime had forced to build the Road of Bones from Magadan to the gold and diamond mines that dotted the area. Just about every building was derelict. I knocked on the door of a hut beside a petrol station. An emaciated, pale young man and his toothless father opened the door and eyed me with suspicion.

'Hello. *Strasvitye*,' I said. 'Uh, good to see you. We have three *mototsikl* on the other side of the river and we need a truck to get across the river. Can you help? I'm English . . . er . . . *Inglesky*.'

The young lad gabbled something in Russian.

'Yeah, yeah . . . ,' I said. 'On the other side of the river. Three *mototsikl* and we want to get across.'

More Russian, this time from the toothless one.

'Yeah, just here . . . it's too big for us . . . no bridge . . . no . . . do you know if there's a *benzin* here?'

They pointed at what I had guessed might be the petrol station.

'Okay, thank you. Do you know if there's like a truck or something that can get across?'

They looked at me blankly again.

Just as I was about to walk away, the young lad beckoned me into his toothless father's car, a back-firing old Lada that was fit only for the scrapheap, and drove me around to someone who fixed passing trucks. He couldn't help, so I returned to our camp on the

Top row, left to right: Truck driver Vladimir, David and Mongolian fixer Kostya.
Bottom row: Vasiliy, Charley, Ewan, Claudio, Russ and Sergey.

River crossings on the Road of Bones united the whole team as we all had to work together to get the bikes, cars and equipment across safely.

or not to cross. We watched them shouting and waving their arms at each other. Then one of them jumped into an articulated truck used for carrying lengths of timber. He gunned the engine and the 30-ton truck lurched into the water. The cab twisted in the water, looking as if it was going to be swept away. Only the rear section, which was anchored on the bank, was preventing it from being washed downstream. Just when we thought the driver was about to lose control, one of the other truck drivers on the far side dragged the logging truck out of the river using a length of steel cable linking the two trucks. That lumber truck was stronger and heavier than either of ours, yet it had been tossed around in the river like a feather in the wind. The implication was clear.

EWAN: The river level had dropped by about 3 feet overnight, so our bank was now too high to breach from the river. We set to work with spades and pickaxes, chipping away at the Road of Bones to construct a gentler slope.

'Look at everyone,' I said to Charley. Ahead of us, Russ, David, Jimmy, Sergey and Vasiliy were cutting away at the riverbank. It was hard work and it was raining. We should have been miserable, but everyone was having a great time.

'If we hadn't decided to do this thing, none of these people would be here now,' I said. 'And Vladimir and the other truck driver wouldn't be here with a job to do and we would never have met most of these people.' It felt wonderful, magical.

An hour or so later, we had finished our ramp and the lumber truck drivers had another go. This time they made it. Then it was our turn. Vladimir engaged the lowest gear and the Kamaz dipped into the river, crawled through the water and climbed the far riverbank like a tortoise hauling itself up a rock. The Warrior was pulled through on a cable, David shouting with alarm as the current threatened to sweep the car downstream.

We'd asked the lumber truck drivers about the state of the roads ahead. They told us there would be hundreds of rivers to cross before we reached Tomtor. I looked quizzically at Vladimir, but he just tapped the side of his neck with his fingers: the Russian sign for vodka, meaning the lumber truck drivers were blind drunk and not to be trusted. Sure enough, Vladimir was right and we sailed through to Tomtor, easily crossing a few shallow rivers on our bikes.

Along the way, Vladimir spotted a baby brown bear and shot it, not because it was a threat but because its fur was worth $600. I was appalled. The loggers we had just encountered were illegally felling trees simply because they would get $100 for each tree trunk. I understood that their lives were not easy and that they might need the money, but it still didn't make it right. Charley was also bitterly disappointed the bear had been shot, not because of the mindless waste of an animal's life but because he'd not seen Vladimir

do it. 'You should have let me shoot it,' he wailed. Again, I was appalled and the arguments on the rights and wrongs of shooting wild animals kept us busy for days afterwards.

Over the next three days, we crossed dozens of rivers, felled trees to fill in ditches and slowly ground our way towards Magadan. We rode for sixteen hours on the first day out of Tomtor, the most exciting sixteen hours of motorcycling I'd ever experienced. The roads deteriorated as we wound our way through mud, gravel, puddles, potholes, rivers and bogs. Just about everything was thrown at us all at once. But all I could think was how much easier it was than I had expected.

But then things started to go badly wrong. First, Charley injured his back. His bike slipped as he was taking it down from the centre stand and, thinking he was going to trap his leg between his falling bike and Claudio's, he tried to wrench it upwards, pulling the muscles behind his shoulder blade. He was in agony and couldn't ride. Second, we'd reached rivers that were too deep to cross. With heavy hearts we had to concede that the rivers had beaten us. They were simply too high to cross in June. We loaded the bikes on the Kamaz and hitched a lift in the support vehicles, Charley dosed to the eyeballs on Vasiliy's painkillers. Within fifteen minutes I knew we'd made the right decision as we bumped through potholes the size of lakes. Even so, we still had a major challenge ahead of us: the river that all the other truck drivers told us even the Kamaz and Ural struggle to cross.

On 25 June, we reached the *big river*, the one we had been warned about. The mother of all river crossings. Vladimir just shook his head and said: 'We wait until tomorrow.' His decision was final. The river was about 300 metres wide and fast flowing, with whole trees floating past. We camped on the riverbank, near the rusting hulk of a bus. Charley and Vladimir stayed up late, drinking vodka into the night. Charley had grown very fond of the Russian, calling him his surrogate father, and I woke at four o'clock in the morning to hear them singing drunkenly.

The next morning, Charley looked dreadful. With Nat King Cole singing that we'd find life was still worthwhile if we just smiled from the Warrior's stereo, the rest of us began chipping away at the riverbank, while Charley looked on. After a couple of hours' digging, the ramp was ready. The Kamaz inched its way into the water and we jumped onto its back. Trembling in the current, it carried us to the far riverbank, where we climbed over the cab and jumped on to the shore to begin working away at that section of the road. Another hour or so later we'd smoothed the lip of the drop sufficiently to enable the Kamaz to climb up on to dry ground.

'Yeaaaaaahhhhhh!' It was Charley, his arms outstretched, high in the air in defiance of his injured shoulder. 'We've fucking done it!' Tears were rolling down his face. We all threw our arms around each other. The unconquerable had been breached. Three and a half weeks after we'd left Ulaanbaatar we'd crossed Siberia. The last big river on the feared and fabled Road of Bones was behind us.

We unloaded the bikes from the Kamaz. Vladimir gave Charley and me the thumbs up, waved us up the road as if to say be gone with you and turned around to return across the river to pick up the support vehicles.

We camped on a hill, the support crew and the truck drivers arriving a little later. For Vladimir, the job was done. He cracked open a bottle of vodka and in a very short space of time became very drunk. It was time to celebrate. And my God, he got plastered. I'd not seen anyone that rubbered for a very long time.

Charley broke down in tears again the next morning when he had to say goodbye to Vladimir. After a round of hugs, we rode nearly four hundred miles on dirt tracks to Karamken and camped that night surrounded by mosquitoes that circled us like a halo and got everywhere. Every second mouthful of dinner that night had one of the little critters in it.

We woke early the next morning to find hoar frost on our tents and our breath condensing in the cold air. It was 28 June and we were about to ride the last few miles to Magadan, one day ahead of schedule. We ate breakfast quickly, packed up and set off by seven o'clock. On the way, we passed a truck that had crashed into the ditch by the side of the road. We climbed up on to it to take a picture before realising the driver was inside the cab.

'*Harosho*? Okay?' I shouted in.

'*Normalya*!' came the reply, with a wave that said get lost.

About five miles from Magadan, I stood up on my pegs, punched the air and screamed my lungs raw. We'd done it! From London right across Europe and Asia to the Pacific. I felt like Valentino Rossi winning a Moto GP. Elated. And then, as we came around a hill, Magadan suddenly revealed itself in the valley below. I stopped my bike at the Mask of Sorrow, a memorial to the victims of Stalin's prison camps, and climbed off. I felt numb. Charley and I walked over to the edge of a ledge that overlooked Magadan and sat down. Resting our chins on the handrail and with our legs dangling over the side, we stared in silence at the city below and the sea beyond. The last time we'd seen open sea, it had been the English Channel and we'd slipped underneath it in a train. Now here was the Pacific ahead of us. It didn't seem real.

Charley and I sat there for almost an hour, just letting our memories of the journey wash over us. We'd survived and relished every experience and not fallen out seriously once. Then we got on our bikes for the last time in Asia and rode into Magadan. As we pulled up outside our hotel, I turned to Charley and pointed at the watch on my wrist.

'You know what time it is?' I said.

'What?' Charley answered.

Since 14 April, the day we had left London, we'd had ambitions of setting off early in the morning, riding until mid-afternoon, and then pitching our tents early enough to give us time to look around, do a bit of fishing or go for a walk. In seventy-six days, we'd not managed it once.

'It's three o'clock,' I said. '*Three o'clock*. On the very last day, we left early and we finished at three o'clock. Can you believe it?'

Right: Relieved to have made it. The statue behind us commemorates the millions of Russians who died while constructing the Road of Bones (which runs from Yakutsk to Magadan) during Stalin's reign of terror.

At Magadan airport with Claudio.

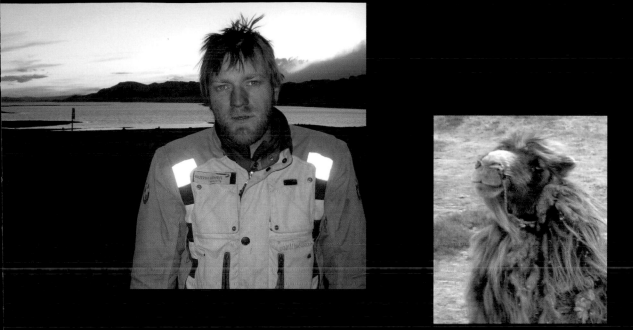

the joys of the open road ...

11 ▶ ▶ ▶

▶ ▶ ▶

Tears in my helmet

ANCHORAGE TO NEW YORK

13,241

MILES

EWAN: Arriving in Alaska was a complete shock. I'd half expected Anchorage to be a romantic, rustic frontier town. Instead it was just like any other American city, with shopping malls, big buildings on a grid of streets and traffic lights at every corner. It felt strange to be back in a place where *everything* was on offer. Having spent two and a half months revelling in the liberation from the most excessive aspects of western consumerism, one of the first things we did on arrival in Anchorage was to succumb immediately to the attractions of an American breakfast. Charley had stuffed French toast and I had Eggs Benedict, with side orders of crispy bacon, lots of orange juice and strong coffee. 'I'm not even hungry,' Charley said, tucking into his breakfast with relish.

We spent four days recuperating in Anchorage, going on trips to see bears and killer whales in the wild, watching television and really appreciating the big, comfortable beds in the hotels. But I found it difficult to shake off a hankering for being in the middle of nowhere. I missed the Road of Bones. I'd never been anywhere else that felt that remote and it had made me feel very comfortable. I yearned for the quiet and the easy camaraderie we had in Siberia, a sense of being able to do exactly what I wanted to do. I'd gone in search of adventure and an alien culture. I'd found both and now I wanted more.

One of the real treats in Alaska was taking our bikes into The Motorcycle Shop in Anchorage for a full service. The shop was run by genuine bikers, lovely guys who sold all different kinds of machines and did a fantastic job with ours. In Anchorage, long-distance bikers were ten a penny; it took a lot to impress them. Every week, they'd see a few bikes arrive in town having finished the Pan-American Highway, a ribbon of more than sixteen thousand miles of continuous road from the tip of South America up to Alaska. We told them we'd come across the water from Siberia.

'We don't see too many who've come from the west,' said the bike shop owner, taking a bit more interest. Then he saw the BMW jacket that Charley had worn from London to Magadan. For seventy-nine days it had been splattered with mud, dust and dirt. It had been washed in streams, showers and hotel baths. When we had started out, it had been bright red with dark and light grey panels. The red had now faded to a pale washed-out orange. The dark grey panels were now light grey. And the previously light grey panels were a sludgy brown – the dirt would no longer wash out.

'Now *that* is impressive,' the bike shop owner said.

On 5 July we set off for New York, riding up towards Fairbanks, where forest fires were encroaching on the city limits and the local population was facing evacuation.

Long before we reached Fairbanks, we could smell the fires in the air. Once we got near, we spoke to some of the firefighters who were slowly bringing more than 1.8 million burning acres under control. There was a huge camp, with tents everywhere and helicopters flying in and out, carrying water to the fires, and it was really exciting to see it.

The next day we entered the Rocky Mountains and spotted a moose casually grazing beside a pond. A little later, I had to disappear into the forest to answer a call of nature. I was in there, doing my business, when I heard Charley and Claudio shouting 'Fucking hell!' I thought nothing of it until I came back out of the woods to see Charley and Claudio looking quite concerned. While I'd been squatting out of sight, a bear had emerged from the forest, very near to where I'd disappeared, and walked right past them.

The roads were wonderful, especially as we'd replaced the knobblies that had carried us across Europe and Asia with soft road tyres. They made the ride much more comfortable and enjoyable on twisty, high-speed roads. It was a revelation to rediscover the pleasures of riding a good bike on good roads. It was also a treat to meet a lot of other bikers who had ridden for long distances. We met a couple in the early stages of a round-the-world trip that was much longer than ours. And we met an old guy called Harold on a 1978 BMW touring bike, who had ridden 875 miles the previous day. By the time he thought about stopping, it was three o'clock in the morning, so he felt he might as well

'It was a revelation to rediscover
the pleasures of riding a good bike
on good roads.'

EWAN

carry on. Harold put us to shame. We'd been moaning after three hundred miles in a day and Harold had done almost three times that distance. The only downside to the excellent roads was the traffic. Compared with Siberia, the roads were teeming with vehicles: hundreds of camper vans, or RVs, and just as many heavy trucks.

And as we rode into more familiar surroundings, the outside world increasingly encroached. For the first time since Slovakia we were easily contactable on the road. Mobile phones worked just about everywhere and consequently the pressures of work started to creep back in. I'd already started reading scripts that had been sent to me when we were in Kazakhstan and Mongolia, but back then I'd found it very difficult to make them mean much to me. Being in my trailer, waiting for the knock on the door and 'Five minutes, Mr McGregor' seemed like another world. Now I was taking calls from directors and agents and the idea of working again had become quite exciting. I could feel that, as we approached the end of our journey, the reality of nearly being home would coincide with looking forward to returning to work. I'd cleared my mind and I felt ready to go back to filming.

Charley was also missing the wilderness. 'I just feel a bit down about the fact that we are back in civilisation and staying in motels,' he said. 'I miss the adventure we had in Kazakhstan, Mongolia and Siberia.'

Maybe it was the absence of a challenge that made it feel so different. We'd been told that mountaineers who conquered Everest always warned that the accidents happened on the way down, when the toughest part of the journey was done and they'd dropped their guard. Jamie Lowther-Pinkerton had warned us that America was the most dangerous country on our itinerary, but, provided we didn't make any mistakes, there was no reason to assume we wouldn't arrive in New York bang on time and in good shape.

On 13 July, having stopped at Dawson Creek in British Columbia, we went in search of pizza. We found a restaurant with a bar and I was outside, smoking a cigarette, when a young guy approached me. He was slightly drunk, a little bit camp and his shirt was unbuttoned to his navel.

'Ewan McGregor,' he said.

'Uh, yeah . . . yeah,' I said.

He asked what we were doing so I told him about our journey. He talked about the Calgary stampede and all the cow girls there.

'I'm married, you know,' I said.

'Oh yeah, shit, yeah right,' he said, smirking. 'You've been away on a motorbike trip for three and a half months and you're married and you mean to tell me that's stopped you . . . ?'

I was really offended. We chatted a bit more, but it wasn't the same. He told me he owned a buffalo farm, but frankly I didn't really care much for his company any more. Pissed off, I went back inside the restaurant and sat down to an enormous pizza with Charley.

A little later, the buffalo farmer came up again and started chatting with Charley. They hit it off and I came to realise he was actually a really sweet guy. His name was Jason, he was great company, very genuine and quite a colourful character. If it hadn't been for Charley, I probably wouldn't have spoken to Jason again, but listening to him I realised that in many ways Jason was just like Charley: very gregarious with a take-me-as-I-am attitude that could be a bit disarming at first.

The next morning, we rode over to Jason's farm. It was a beautiful huge ranch, with great big red barns. He had reared three buffalo from calves, bottle-feeding them because their mothers had died. These buffalo were now mature, but they had become pets. I'd never been up close to one, but he let us sit on one called Lucy, who took quite a shine to Claudio, nudging him in the groin as he tried to film us riding on her back.

Having arranged to meet Jason a few days later in Calgary, we headed off south again. We were averaging three hundred miles a day and the accumulated exhaustion of fourteen weeks in the saddle was starting to take its toll. Several times each day I would find myself falling asleep at the handlebars, unable to keep my eyes open on the bike. The only remedy was to stop and lie down on the side of the road for a few minutes. I was dying to get to New York to see my wife. More than anything I just wanted to put my arms round her, but I was also desperate for a rest.

Two days later, we were approaching Calgary. It was early afternoon and we had a good lunch in our bellies, Charley was riding at the front with Claudio and I was at the back. Wearing jeans, T-shirts and leather or canvas jackets, we were riding up towards the brow of a hill when the traffic ahead of us slowed suddenly. Charley put his hazard lights on. Riding at about 60mph, I reached forward to put my hazard lights on too. There was a screech of tyres and then the bike went completely out of control. It happened so fast, I don't know which came first. Charley said afterwards that he saw it all in his wing mirrors.

'Out of nowhere, a red car just whammed into the back of you,' he said afterwards. 'Your front wheel went straight up in the air, almost vertical, then slammed down on the road. You were all over the place, your handlebars weaving from right to left to right to left. Somehow, you managed to stay on and come to a stop.'

Outside Calgary.

All I could remember was a bang, suddenly being out of control, seeing a big grass ditch about 6 feet deep to my left and thinking I was going to topple into it.

I'm not going on the grass, I'm not going on the grass, I repeated to myself and managed to pull the bike round. The next thing I noticed was that my bike was still running after being smashed in the tail end, that I was still on it and that it was riding straight and true.

I pulled off to the side of the highway, put my bike on its side stand and got off unharmed, unscathed. Fuck, this bike is amazing, I thought. I've just been hit from behind and I managed to ride in a straight line. It could have been very nasty, but I came away without a scratch.

'I was hit!' I said to Charley as I walked past him towards the car that had tail-ended me.

'I know,' he said.

A kid, about seventeen years old, dressed in big baggy pants with a chain wallet, got out of a red Honda Civic. The poor kid was in a bit of a state and his car was wrecked. The bonnet was crumpled. The front grill and the mudguard were lying on the ground.

'What were you doing with your eyes?' I asked.

'I didn't see you, man,' he replied.

Charley was furious. 'What the fuck are you doing?' he screamed at the kid. 'You almost killed my friend!'

'It's fine. It was just an accident and accidents happen,' I said. 'Are you all right?'

'Yeah, yeah. I'm all right, man,' he said.

Then he turned around. 'Oh, my fucking car's fucked, man. My fucking car's fucking fucked.' All I could think was that I was lucky to be alive and he was worrying about his car!

Meanwhile, I was as high as a kite. The adrenalin was pumping and I felt elated. We looked at the back of my bike. My pannier boxes had crumpled and the pannier frame was broken in two places. Protruding about 4 inches behind the back tyre, the panniers had saved my life, absorbing the impact that otherwise would've been straight on to my back wheel. There was no question that I would have hit the deck and slipped under the car if he had hit my rear wheel. It would have stopped it dead and I would have been run over, probably crushed under the bike beneath the car. In all likelihood, it would have killed me. We'd come through some of the most difficult road conditions in the world and our first accident was someone tail-ending me on a Canadian highway . . .

I felt so sorry for the wee guy. When the police turned up, he didn't even know which document was his insurance policy. Nevertheless, it was difficult to understand how he hadn't managed to see me.

I got back on my bike and rode off. Charley was behind me and I felt a real bond with him there. I could feel him looking out for me. He knew that after an accident I'd be a bit shaky for a wee while and he was watching over me. As we approached Calgary the adrenalin wore off and depression set in. Thoughts raced through my mind of what might've been. We got to the hotel and I had a bath. As I lay in the tub, I felt my spirits rise again. It was as if I'd been given a second chance. I felt extraordinarily alive. I felt great.

We went out for dinner that night. Arriving at the restaurant, I felt on top of the world, really buzzing, chatting away to the waitress. It was so unlike me, but I was still as high as a kite. We had a fantastic steak dinner, everything sparkled and everybody was great company. Charley got a bit drunk and started making speeches about how much he loved everybody at the table. He went on at length about how much Claudio meant to him and how we couldn't have done the trip without him. I could see the red wine in his eyes and, of course, when someone mentioned it the next day, he tried to brush it off.

'Yeah, it was nothing,' he said with a grin. 'I was just a bit pissed.' Then he looked a bit more serious than usual. 'No, actually I meant every word of it.'

CHARLEY: Next day we got Ewan's bike and panniers repaired at the biggest bike shop any of us had ever seen. They did a fabulous job and, by chance, there was a stunt rider at the garage. He did some stunts for us outside, a couple of tyre burns, some stand-up wheelies, sitting on the tank wheelies and some stoppies. Afterwards, we jumped on our bikes and somebody shouted: 'Go on then, do a wheelie.' With most of the bike shop employees watching, I was very nervous, but I still popped a beauty, a nice long wheelie along the road.

That evening, we met Jason, the buffalo farmer, in a bar and had a few drinks. 'It's the best fun you'll have with your boots on,' he said as we headed off to the stampede, where I promptly lost Ewan and had to borrow money from Jason all evening. My wallet had been stolen a week earlier, when we had stopped off for a dip in some natural hot springs. Claudio had had a bag stolen in Russia, but Ewan and I had travelled all the way through some of the poorest countries in Europe and Asia without having anything stolen. It was my fault for not taking more care and putting my wallet in one of the lockers, but I'd lowered my guard once we'd arrived in North America, thinking that I was less likely to have something stolen. Strangely, the gypsy in Prague had said that I would lose some money before the end of the trip.

We rode on to the American frontier, our last border crossing. Having crossed frontiers into France, Belgium, Germany, the Czech Republic, Slovakia, the Ukraine, Russia several times, Kazakhstan, Mongolia and Canada, we thought we had borders sussed. We passed through the Canadian section without a hitch and carried on to the American boundary. About 20 yards short of the huts, Ewan and I stopped to take off our helmets while we waited for David and Jimmy in the support vehicle. Immediately, a female American border guard came running out and screamed at us.

'You cannot stop there!' she shouted. 'You *cannot* stop there! Proceed through the checks! You cannot stop *there*!'

'Uh, we're just waiting for our . . . we're just waiting for our friends,' I said.

'You have to go back. You have to wait back there. You cannot stop,' she said. The idea that two guys on motorbikes were a major security threat was daft, but, more than anything, we were embarrassed for her. She was making such an arse of herself, screaming and shouting. It freaked me out, so I jumped back on my bike, turned round and rode back as she had told us.

'That's a one-way road!' she shouted. 'You cannot go back there!'

Behind me, Ewan was facing her down. 'Calm down,' he said. 'He's going back because you just said we had to go back.'

'No, you have to clear the American border and then if you want to go back . . .'

'Listen, he's going back because you just told us to go back.'

'I did not tell you!'

Claudio and Ewan gave up. They rode up to the checkpoint, where the border guard treated them like dirt until she asked why they had a carnet. As soon as they explained that they had filming equipment in the support car, her behaviour changed. She became a little kitten, putty in our hands. It was equally embarrassing to see her behave in such an obsequious manner. We got through the checks, hugged each other because it was our last border crossing, and set off into Montana.

As we rode into America, I realised I was fulfilling a dream I'd had since I was a teenager: to ride across America on a motorbike. I'd been so focused on our final target of New York, that it had taken two weeks on the smooth roads of North America before it dawned on me that one of my longest-held dreams was coming true.

But mixed with my joy was disappointment that the journey was approaching its end. We'd had difficult times, but we'd come through them stronger than before. My biggest worry had been that the stresses of the journey would drive Ewan and me apart. In many ways we were chalk and cheese, but we'd come to respect the differences and love what we had in common. I felt very lucky to have emerged from the trip having gained so much.

Montana was fabulous, with beautiful scenery. We stopped off for one day at the ranch belonging to the guy who was the inspiration for the film *The Horse Whisperer*. After a big supper, we had a great night's sleep and the next morning we were invited to see the horse whisperer train a horse. It was great to see this man at work. He was so light and in tune with the animals. Afterwards, we helped round up some horses and lasso a cow, then we sat down to a delicious lunch before setting off for the long ride west. Passing through Native American country, it was difficult not to draw comparisons with Mongolia. Like the Mongolian herdsmen, the Native Americans of the Great Plains had been nomadic, living in tepees and moving on to follow the buffalo herds and find their animals fresh pasture to graze. The difference was that the nomadic lifestyle was still fully operational in Mongolia, whereas the white man had stopped the Native Americans from living the way that they and thousands of other people had lived for a very long time.

'Why was it possible in Mongolia, but not in America?' Ewan asked. He was really angered by the unjust way the Native Americans had been treated. 'It's a wide open country and it's just not right.'

We rode on via Rapid City, a charming place like a town from a Frank Capra movie, to Waseca in Minnesota. It was a long ride under the big skies of South Dakota, interrupted only by stop-offs at Mount Rushmore and the Little Big Horn, the scene of Custer's last stand. By the time we reached Waseca we had ridden 542 miles. Fuelled by

...a long ride under big skies

Mountain Dew Amp, a high-energy drink, it set the one-day record for the trip. In Waseca, we stayed with Chantelle, the sister of Kyle, the American embassy employee we'd met while he was surveying military radio installations in Mongolia. Kyle had given me a little medallion for his sister. Having carried it halfway around the world from Mongolia, I was determined to get it to her. Chantelle and her husband were lovely. They put us up, gave us breakfast, the first home-cooked meal we'd had since we had been in a ger in Mongolia, and the next day showed us around their large arable farm, letting us climb over their massive John Deere tractors like little boys.

From Waseca, we rode via Madison to Chicago, stopping off at the Harley-Davidson factory along the way. Arriving at the factory on three dusty, slightly damaged BMWs that had been around the world was great. We lined up beside the rows of gleaming Harleys, mostly belonging to employees, and felt very proud. They showed us around the plant, where we watched an engine being built, travelling along the factory production line, being customised to the purchaser's requirement. For Ewan and me it was like letting children loose in a sweetshop. At the end of the line, a lovely lady plugged in the engine and fired it up. Bam! It started up straightaway and we'd just witnessed the woman giving birth to the engine. It made us feel like getting out the cigars and celebrating.

Afterwards, they let us ride a couple of Harleys. I'd never been a great fan, thinking Harleys weren't really suited to the British climate, but I could absolutely see the point in the States, where they were ideal for cruising in a long, straight line in T-shirt and shades.

EWAN: The next day we followed Jimmy's dad on his Kawasaki cruiser from our hotel in Chicago back to his house in the suburbs of the city for lunch with Jimmy's family. Living in a comfortable all-American neighbourhood, where most of the houses had a veranda and an American flag flying outside, they'd laid on a fantastic spread, which we ate out on the balcony while Claudio played ragtime on the piano. That evening, David and I went to see *Frankie and Johnny in the Clair de Lune* at the Steppenwolf Theatre Company, where John Malkovich had started out. I'd been gagging to see some theatre and it was just gorgeous, a great production. I was so excited to be sitting back in a theatre. When the lights went down, I knew it was time to get back to work. The ride across America had become a decompression chamber from the isolation of Mongolia and Siberia and I felt as if I was at last ready to come up for air. It was really good for me to go and see a great play, particularly as it was completely by chance. All I'd known was that I wanted to see a Steppenwolf production. We went along, picked up the tickets and it just happened to be a phenomenal play with a great cast. We had dinner afterwards and then went to two busy bars where some great blues was being played.

I went to bed very satisfied with my evening and hungry to get back to work.

The next day, my wife and Charley's family arrived in New York. Eve was now only seven hundred miles and one time zone away, the closest we'd been for three months. I was very excited about finishing the journey and seeing her again, but also strangely nervous. Although we'd spoken almost daily, we'd lived separate lives for a quarter of a year and we'd got used to existing day to day on our own.

Before we were reunited with our families in New York, we each had one last treat planned. Charley wanted to visit an amusement park that was home to some of the world's highest and longest rollercoasters – not my idea of fun – and I wanted to visit Orange County Choppers.

Just before we left Chicago, Charley got a note from David. 'I know the time in New York might fly by without a chance to say that this has been a thing of incredible beauty to me on every level,' it said. 'Thank you for letting me be a part of it, I'm crying and I don't know why and I don't want to stop. Dave.'

One of the reasons it would be so difficult to end the trip in a few days' time in New York was that it would mean we'd all go our separate ways. Without David and Russ's complete devotion, the trip wouldn't have turned out such a great success. Charley and I were both really touched by what David and Russ had done for us. Starting out just as business associates, we'd come to respect each other and in the course of the journey we'd become the closest of friends, forming a relationship we'd treasure and cherish for the rest of our lives. We'd started out as colleagues and ended up a band of brothers.

But it wasn't just David, Russ, Jimmy, Claudio and Charley who felt special to me. I had also fallen in love with my bike. The next day I was standing outside a motel, smoking a cigarette, and I looked at my BMW. I felt really sad. It looked so fantastic and yet I'd soon have to say goodbye to it. I stood beside it for ages, smoking one cigarette after another, just staring at it like some infatuated lover. I was so proud of it. It looked awesome and it looked like it had gone round the world for the simple reason that it really had.

For the next couple of days just about everything we did – the last full tank of petrol, the last night Charley, Claudio and I spent on our own, the last long day's ride – was tinged with a mixture of sadness and excitement. On the evening of 27 July, we passed a signpost that read 'New York 166 Miles'. We tapped 'hotel' into the GPS and were led to The Chestnut Inn on Oquaga Lake in upper New York State. It was a beautiful place, just the right setting for Charley, Claudio and I to have our last meal together. As we sat down for dinner, I realised I had no regrets over the trip. Sure, there'd been hard times, but they had always led to good times. And the hard times were the ones that I was likely to remember most fondly.

This trip wasn't just about riding two great bikes through some of the world's most remote landscapes; it was about the people we met along the way.

The next day, we rode about eighty miles to Orange County Choppers in Montgomery. Eighteen months earlier, when I'd been busy with work, I'd whiled away the downtime in my trailer, waiting to get on to a film set, by watching the first series of Orange County Choppers on DVD. It became an obsession and after a while I'd be itching to finish a take so that I could get back to my trailer and watch some more of the show. 'Okay, are we done?' I'd say. 'Right, can I . . . ?' and I'd horse back to the trailer. And by all accounts, I was not the only person hooked on the show about a father–son team – Paul Teutul Senior and Paul Junior – building custom bikes with a third guy, Vinnie, in their workshop and arguing like hell. The show had three million viewers in the States and fifty thousand people turned up to see the Teutuls when they appeared at a bike show. The two Pauls were incredibly friendly and showed us around the workshop. I got our world map out and showed them where we'd been. They were very interested and then they said what I'd been really hoping for: 'Let's go for a ride.'

They gave me a chopper about 12 feet long and on which my backside was lower than the top of the rear wheel. It was ridiculous, but it felt so good. I wheeled it back – you needed to pick your spot if you wanted to do a U-turn – and, not realising it had a big mudguard at the back, I dinged it into the wall. Paul Junior was standing next to me. 'Woah, woah, woah!' he said.

I was mortified. Fortunately, I'd not chipped the beautiful paint job. Charley was such a sports bike rider that I hadn't expected him to be particularly excited by the experience, but when I looked over at him on another chopper I could see he was absolutely thrilled. Sitting on two enormously long bikes, we fired them up and were blown away by the roar of the engines. Their primary belt drives were winging around on the left of the bike,

Above: At the famous Orange County Choppers, New Jersey.
Above left: With Paul Snr., the owner.

terrifying us with the thought we'd get our trouser legs caught in the 3-inch-wide rubber belt. The exhaust pipes on Charley's chopper swept along the side of the bike and then tilted upwards. Whenever he blasted the throttle, my hair would be blown back by the exhaust from his pipes. Paul Senior was riding a Santa Claus bike with Christmas lights and reindeer antlers and his son was on a prisoner-of-war bike, a huge big thing.

We knocked the choppers into first and pulled up a hill that led on to the road. The two Pauls led the way and stopped at the top. Oh, for fuck's sake, don't stop there, I thought. The bikes were worth around $70,000 and I was terrified I was going to drop mine. Charley was in front of me. I was playing with my handlebars a bit and I saw Charley looking down. I was tapping his leg with my front wheel; I hadn't realised it was so far ahead of me.

And then we got out on the road. My chopper felt just fantastic. With 103-cubic-inch V-twin engines, they were much more industrial than our BMWs or a sports bike, and we really had to thwack through the gears, but they just had so much grunty torque. In a straight line, they rode like a dream. You could hear the electric guitars twanging. I looked over at Charley. His long hair was blowing in the wind and he had a smile on his face as big as the Cheshire Cat's, and he suited it. Charley really did. I imagined us by the ocean, cruising through California on those choppers, and I thought that if I ever ended up living in Los Angeles I would definitely get a couple just so that when Charley visited we could go riding along the coastal highway. It looked perfect.

After visiting Orange County Choppers, we rode for about an hour to a beautiful hotel. David had said he wanted us to spend the last night in a special place. We were sitting in a little pagoda, having a drink and chatting about the trip, waiting for our rooms to be ready. Charley had already wondered if Eve, Olly, Doone and Kinvara were already at the hotel, and I suddenly had the strangest feeling that he might be right.

'They're not here, are they, David?' I said. My heart was racing, I had butterflies in my stomach and, all of a sudden, I felt really anxious about seeing Eve again.

David looked really surprised. 'What?' he said.

'The girls; they're not here, are they?' I said.

'No, they're in Manhattan,' David said. 'Why, did you think they might be?'

'No, no . . . I didn't . . . it's just . . . Charley and I . . . it's just I wanted to know if they're here so I can stop my heart beating like this,' I said.

'What do you think it's going to be like when you see your wife for the first time?' David asked.

'Insane. No, it won't be insane. It'll be . . . ,' I said, trying to find the right words, but I was interrupted by a scream.

'Daddy! Daddy! Daddy!' Doone was running across the grass towards us. Kinvara was frozen to the spot, so excited she was unable to move.

'Oh my God,' Charley said.

'Oh my God,' I said.

They were there. I jumped over the railing of the little pagoda thing, ran up to Eve and took her in my arms. It was just the most incredible feeling. A weird, heady, out-of-body feeling of actually seeing Eve in the flesh. I tried to kiss her, but I hadn't trimmed my moustache and beard, so every time I tried to make contact with her lips, I was kissing my own facial hair. It was getting irritating, so I lifted it up to give her a proper kiss. I'd missed it so much.

'I knew you were here,' I said.

'Why?' Eve said, her voice trembling.

'I could just feel your presence. I knew it.'

Eve was obsessed with my beard. She didn't like me with it. 'I want to see it off you!' she said. 'Oh God, it's so bizarre. I know it's you, but it doesn't quite feel like you.'

Charley was hugging and kissing his wife and daughters, going through much the same experience as me, only without the beard in the way. He had a little goatee, but his wife said she quite liked it.

David was watching us all, the look on his face a mixture of sheer joy and slight embarrassment that by now he ought to be somewhere else. 'Ten fingers, ten toes, a little more hair, but otherwise just the same. Now it's over to you, ma'am,' he said to Eve. 'He's back to you and I'm outta here.'

My daughters were with their grandparents in France, so Eve and I walked alone into the hotel. I couldn't stop staring at her and touching her. But by the time we got into the elevator to go up to the room, it felt completely natural to be with Eve, because we do belong together. All the apprehension and anxiety had disappeared. The moment we saw each other again, it just felt right.

That night we all had dinner together and told our families about our adventures. Then we went upstairs. Olly had a terrible headache, so Eve and I went downstairs to a gift shop to get her some aspirin. As we were walking back to the lifts we passed a big ballroom where there was some line dancing going on. I looked in the door. There, in the middle of the dance floor, was Olly with Charley, Doone and Kinvara dancing in a big ring, holding hands. I watched them for a wee while. It looked fantastic. Charley was completely at home again with his family and I could see the excitement on his daughters' faces.

The hotel was a big old building. It had the air of a place to which families went for their summer holiday year after year. But as Eve and I returned to our room, none of it meant anything to me. As far as I was concerned, there were only two guests in the hotel: Eve and me. I climbed into bed with my wife again. It felt so right.

By the next morning, however, I was focused again on the journey. Eating breakfast with Eve, I felt my bike beckoning. And having not seen my wife for nearly four months, I left her sitting at the breakfast table on her own, so that I could head upstairs and sort my bags out. My bike had temporarily become a third party in my marriage and I needed to honour an appointment with her.

A short while later I was sitting in the sun in front of the hotel, my bike packed beside me, thinking back over the trip. Mongolia had been the undisputed highlight. All sorts of things popped into my mind, some of them significant, some of them trivial, like a restaurant in which we ate lunch or somewhere we had to stop for a pee at the side of the road. And the randomness was what was nice about it, I thought, hoping that for the rest of my life the memories would just keep coming back.

What I'd miss most of all was the sense of having a lot of time on our hands. Even on days when we put four or five hundred miles under our wheels, once we'd stopped, parked up and pitched our tents, the rest of the day was ours. And I'd also come to enjoy all the hold-ups and stops, whether it was a rest stop for something to drink or an enforced stop because the Red Devil had broken down. Most times, we'd have a laugh and kick around. Charley and I had already joked about how we would get home and the first weekend one of us would phone the other to arrange a meet at the petrol station on the King's Road, where we'd stand for half an hour kicking stones around. I knew I'd also miss the time for reflection I'd had on the bike.

Charley and I got on the bikes for the last time and immediately became like kids showing off to the girls we fancied at school. We pulled wheelies and other stunts to impress our wives, dying for them to tell us to stop in case we hurt ourselves. David pulled us aside and told us we had to do an interview with someone from BMW on the way to Orange County Choppers, where we were going to meet up with Paul Senior and Paul Junior. An interview was the last thing Charley or I wanted to do, mainly because we were dying to get back to the choppers, which I wanted to show Eve. David said we couldn't get out of it and that he had arranged for us to meet the BMW executive at a coffee shop about ten minutes away. We pulled up as arranged outside the coffee shop in the little town and waited for him. A short while later, we spotted Russ and the executive approaching, both riding BMW bikes. Having not seen Russ for a while, I was really pleased to see him and went up to him as he took his helmet off.

'Great to see you,' I said. 'We really missed you on the last leg.'

'Yeah, me too,' Russ said. 'Let me just introduce Laurence from BMW.'

I turned around. Laurence had his back to me and was taking his helmet off. As he removed it, I suddenly thought, hey, it's Ted Simon, simply because it felt a bit odd to be introduced to someone who had their back to me. The mystery man turned around and for a split second I was speechless, then it just burst out of me: 'Daaaaaaaaaddd!'

I hadn't had the slightest idea my father was going to be there. No inkling at all. It was a brilliant surprise and I was so proud that my dad could join us for the final push. We hugged and kissed, each of us as excited as the other, then set off for Orange County Choppers, where we picked up a few more riders, including Paul Senior, Paul Junior, Vinnie, and some of the mechanics and bike builders, most of them on Harleys rather than their very precious choppers.

With a mixture of heavy hearts and extreme excitement, we moved off for the very

New York. We'd made it.

Below, clockwise from left: Ewan, Claudio's daughters Larissa and Xenia,
Claudio, Charley and Claudio's wife Regina.

last time. Destination: Manhattan. As we rode towards New York beneath a clear blue sky, the emotions of finishing started to snowball in my mind. For a few moments I thought it was all wrong, that it should be just Charley, Claudio and me. I thought that maybe we'd made a mistake riding with about forty other bikers who hadn't seen what we'd seen or done what we'd done, but when I turned around and saw a phalanx of bikes stretching back along the road as far as the eye could see, I realised it was exactly the right thing to be doing. All I really wanted was Charley up next to me, so that the two of us could be side by side, and by the time we got to the George Washington Bridge, Charley had caught up, I had my dad in my rear-view mirror and I was overjoyed that we were surrounded by bikes. Waiting for everyone to pay their toll, I was shaking my head. It was awesome having all the bikes around us. It added to the sense of achievement, which I really felt warranted a procession of noise into the city.

And then we set off. Riding down the ramp on to the bridge, Charley and I stood up on our pegs and the glorious Manhattan skyline suddenly appeared on our right, stretching down the Hudson River. A helicopter was flying level with us over the water, a cameraman hanging out of its door, and I was gone. I burst into tears, crying like a baby, the tears rolling down my face as I blubbed into my helmet and pulled a V for victory sign to the helicopter swooping nearby. All the way across the bridge and halfway down the West Side Highway, the tears kept flowing. I was overwhelmed, looking at the buildings through my tears and thinking we've done it, we've done it, we've done it. I'd been excited about finishing and I was looking forward to the adulation, to people saying 'Well done, you're the business', but I really hadn't expected to feel this way. The noise of all the bikes was deafening. Some of the Orange County bikers were doing burn-outs, great clouds of blue tyre smoke rising into the warm air. At traffic lights, all forty of us would rev our engines to the red line and beep our horns, then race away from the lights when they turned green.

'We did it,' I shouted across to Charley. 'We fucking did it. We wanted to do it. We said we'd do it. We fucking did it.'

At the next traffic lights, Charley leaned over to me. 'I can't really take all this in,' he shouted over the deafening din of the bikes. 'It hasn't really hit me yet that it's nearly all over, but I just want to say it's the best fucking thing I've ever done and I want to thank you for that.'

As we rode away from the lights, I was still in bits and I could feel Charley's love supporting me as we rode through the concrete canyons of New York. Two blocks away from our finishing line at Battery Park, I suddenly thought, shit, I'm going to burn my clutch out a block away from the finish, but I made it into the park. There, standing in

front of me, were loads of friends. I saw Ciara, my publicist, and hugged Lindy, my agent. But more than anything I wanted Eve. I needed to see my wife, but I couldn't find her. I scanned the crowds and then I spotted her on the other side of the fence. I ran over and grabbed her. Again I was gone, weeping into Eve's hair and neck. I was just completely blown away by it. We'd done it, we were there.

Then I had to find Charley. Again I scanned the crowd. There he was. I ran over, threw my arms around him, hugged him tight and buried my head in his shoulder.

'We've done it,' I sobbed into his shoulder. 'We've done it and I love you.' I couldn't get much else out between the sobs.

'Thanks, mate,' Charley said. 'It's been great.' We'd spent fourteen weeks in each other's company and not really fallen out once. 'It could have gone either way,' Charley said. 'We could have ended the journey never wanting to see each other again. But it didn't happen that way. You've become the brother I never had.'

Pulling the corks on two magnums of champagne, we sprayed them all over each other and the onlookers; we were hot and sweaty, our hair was matted and my beard was all over the place. Charley just looked like he'd crawled out of the river.

'You'll never look better in your life,' Ciara shouted over at us, 'because you look exactly like you've done what you've just done.'

We gave a series of interviews and posed for photographs, feeling on top of the world and loving every minute of it. Then Charley, Claudio, my father, Russ and I got back on our bikes and rode up through the streets of Manhattan. It was baking hot and I looked over at my dad. 'Never in my wildest dreams did I think I'd be riding on a motorcycle around Manhattan with you,' I shouted to him. It couldn't have been better.

My father was usually the most law-abiding of bikers, never breaking the speed limit, but he was following us over pavements and cutting across the corners of sidewalks to get round traffic lights. We returned the bikes my father and Russ had been riding to BMW, and then Charley and I took our two beloved bikes around to the Maritime Hotel where the Black Rebel Motorcycle Club were going to play at our homecoming party that evening.

There was a lot still to come. That night we'd go to the party, where I'd have a very strange reaction to seeing our riding suits, helmets and boots displayed in Perspex cabinets as if they were museum pieces – I'd just want to put them back on, get on my bike and head off west to do the whole journey in reverse – and where I'd be blown away by the huge enlarged photographs taken on the trip. It was strange to see the wee faces of the guys at a petrol station in Mongolia and to think that we had been there not very long ago. A few days later, Charley and I would watch our two BMWs being loaded on to a flight from JFK to London. After that, we'd pick them up from Heathrow and ride them the twelve miles from the airport back to Bulwer Street, where we'd finally cross the line we hadn't seen since that warm April morning we'd ridden away from our families and friends. It was important for Charley and me to return to the point at which we'd started, but, that formality aside, the journey was over. We'd made it from London to New York, 18,478 miles 'on the road' according to my odometer, plus several hundred miles by train and a few thousand miles by air.

Outside the Maritime Hotel I unstrapped my luggage and unloaded the panniers from my motorbike, threw them in the back of a yellow New York taxi and stepped inside. It was strangely mundane to be sitting in a taxi on my own after nearly four months with Charley always at my side, but as the taxi bumped along the avenues of New York, somehow it just felt right. Five minutes later, the taxi was standing outside the hotel where I was staying with my wife. I gave the driver a good tip, walked in, took the lift up to our room, ran a bath and lay back in the suds with a contented sigh. At long last, it was done.

22,345

MILES

Appendix A
Route

Date	Destination	Country	Mileage between destinations	Cumulative mileage
week 1				
April 14	Brussels	Belgium	244	244
April 15	Nürburg	Germany	170	414
April 16	Prague	Czech Rep.	428	842
April 17	Prague			842
April 18	Jedovnice		145	987
April 19	Bojnice	Slovakia	128	1115
April 20	Turna Nad Bodvou		146	1261
week 2				
April 21	Uzhhorod	Ukraine	80	1341
April 22	Lviv		153	1494
April 23	Kiev		329	1823
April 24	Kiev			1823
April 25	Kharkiv		295	2118
April 26	Krasnyy Luch		188	2306
April 27	Belaya Kalitva	Russia	125	2431
week 3				
April 28	Volgograd		208	2639
April 29	Volgograd			2639
April 30	Astrakhan		249	2888
May 1	Atyrau	Kazakhstan	223	3111
May 2	Atyrau			3111
May 3	20 miles south of Qandyaghash		305	3416
May 4	50 miles south of Qarabutaq		268	3684
week 4				
May 5	Aral Sea		160	3844
May 6	Qyzylorda		298	4142
May 7	Shymkent (Cimkent)		271	4413
May 8	Almaty		419	4832
May 9	Almaty			4832
May 10	Almaty			4832
May 11	Almaty			4832

	Destination	Country	Mileage between destinations	Cumulative mileage
week 5				
May 12	Charyn Canyon		113	4945
May 13	15 miles west of Kalinino		158	5103
May 14	Ayaköz		379	5482
May 15	Semey (Semipalatinsk)		221	5703
May 16	Barnaul	Russia	274	5977
May 17	Gorno-Altaysk		159	6136
May 18	Tashanta		314	6450
week 6				
May 19	Tsagannuur	Mongolia	33	6483
May 20	5 miles south of Hotgor		110	6593
May 21	Ulaangom		64	6657
May 22	Uvs Lake		36	6693
May 23	Baruunturuun		67	6760
May 24	Ondorhangay		39	6799
May 25	Lake Telmen		94	6893
May 26	White Lake		169	7062
week 7				
May 27	White Lake			7062
May 28	Kharkhorin (Kharakorum)		168	7230
May 29	Ulaanbaatar		240	7470
May 30	Ulaanbaatar			7470
May 31	Ulaanbaatar			7470
June 1	Ulaanbaatar			7470
week 8				
June 2	Ulan Ude	Russia	340	7810
June 3	Ulan Ude			7810
June 4	Ulan Ude			7810
June 5	Ulan Ude			7810
June 6	Khilok		210	8020
June 7	Chita		203	8223
June 8	on train (from Chita via Skovorodino)		580	8803

	Destination	Country	Mileage between destinations	Cumulative mileage
week 9				
June 9	15 miles north of Tynda		132	8935
June 10	Tynda		15	8950
June 11	Tynda			8950
June 12	Nagornyy		60	9010
June 13	10 miles north of Tommot		286	9296
June 14	Yakutsk		270	9566
June 15	Yakutsk			9566
week 10				
June 16	Yakutsk			9566
June 17	Matta		48	9614
June 18	Chamnayy		151	9765
June 19	on ferry heading for Khandyga		56	9821
June 20	20 miles east of Khandyga		36	9857
June 21	30 miles west of Tomtor		236	10,093
June 22	Tomtor		30	10,123
week 11				
June 23	Tomtor			10,123
June 24	20 miles east of Kuranakh-Sala		69	10,192
June 25	20 miles west of Adygalakh		35	10,227
June 26	Kadykchan		58	10,285
June 27	Karamken		390	10,675
June 28	Magadan		61	10,736
June 29	Magadan			10,736
week 12				
June 30	Magadan			10,736
July 1 (i)	In flight Magadan–Anchorage (crossing IDL)			
July 1 (ii)	Anchorage, AK	USA	2505	13,241
July 2	Anchorage			13,241
July 3	Anchorage			13,241
July 4	Anchorage			13,241
July 5	Anderson, AK		292	13,533

	Destination	Country	Mileage between destinations	Cumulative mileage
week 13				
July 6	Fox, AK		89	13,622
July 7	Tok, AK		214	13,836
July 8	Burwash Landing, YT	Canada	212	14,048
July 9	Whitehorse, YT		174	14,222
July 10	Whitehorse			14,222
July 11	Watson Lake, YT		274	14,496
July 12	Fort Nelson, BC		326	14,822
week 14				
July 13	Dawson Creek, BC		284	15,106
July 14	Edmonton, AB		360	15,466
July 15	Calgary, AB		189	15,655
July 16	Calgary			15,655
July 17	Libby, MT	USA	383	16,038
July 18	Columbia Falls, MT		104	16,142
July 19	Billings, MT		483	16,625
week 15				
July 20	Rapid City, SD		374	16,999
July 21	Waseca, MN		542	17,541
July 22	Madison, WI		267	17,808
July 23	Chicago, IL		148	17,956
July 24	Chicago, IL			17,956
July 25	Lagrange, IN		143	18,099
July 26	Warren, OH		259	18,358
week 16				
July 27	Oquaga Lake, Deposit, NY		353	18,711
July 28	Rock Tavern, NY		102	18,813
July 29	New York City		74	18,887
	to London		3458	22,345

Appendix B

Equipment

Modifications and additions to Ewan's and Charley's BMW GS 1150 Adventures

All by Touratech: Zega pannier system, Remus exhaust system, steering stop, headlight cover, sump guard, wide foot pegs, rally mudguard, additional fog headlight pair, oil-cooler guard, ROK all-purpose flat straps, cigarette lighter sockets, accessory sockets, power data lead, lockable GPS brackets, windscreen spoiler, handguard spoiler, 2l holder and canister for panniers, pannier inner bags, Arno stretch bands, tool kits, tyre puncture repair kit, Ortlieb dry bags, Cascade compression bags.

AirHawk seat cushions.

Camping equipment

One of the following: Northface three-man tent, Northface one-man tent, Coleman Viper one-man tent. CamelBak, tent lamp, torch, toilet roll holder.

Two of the following: Touratech tent bags, large packsacks, Pack-it All Aboard II, Poly Survival Bags, bivvy bags, Mountain Equipment Snowline sleeping bags, sleeping-bag inners, Thermarest chair kits, Thermarest mats, collapsible aluminium stools, mosquito head nets, fishing bags, tackle boxes, Giant Soft Fibre Trek towels, drysacks and assorted stuff sacks.

Cooking

Optimus stoves, firesteels, MSR fuel and water bottles, Ortlieb folding bowl, polythene drinks bottles 0.5l, polythene drinks bottles 1l, Aladdin flasks 0.5l, titanium cutlery sets, titanium mugs, Miniworks water filter and maintenance kit, tea towels, heavy duty wiresaws, survival tins, ten disposable lighters, MSR Alpine Classic Cook set, MSR Mini Cook set, can opener, salt and pepper, curry and herbs, cooking oil, OXO cubes (mixed), Tabasco sauce, skimmed milk powder, Bovril, Marmite, cordial.

Food

Camping meals, rice, couscous, pasta, Supa noodles, cereal bars, dried fruit, Oatso Simple (assorted flavours), packet soups, sweets, chocolate, Kendal Mint Cake.

Personal items

Mosquito repellent jacket, mosquito repellent trousers, Belstaff jackets, Gore-Tex® jackets, Gore-Tex® trousers, fleece jackets, lightweight trousers, canvas shorts, sweatshirts, short-sleeve shirts, T-shirts, silk long johns, underwear, hiking socks, walking boots, hat, snoods, sunglasses, wristwatches, eye masks, travel soap, dry wash, toothbrush, toothpaste, razors and blades, shaving gel, moisturiser, lip salve, sun protection – factor 30, baby wipes, hand sanitiser, soap, soap dish, shower gel, shampoo, 100 per cent deet, Berocca, antacid tablets,

multivitamins, cod liver oil tablets, aspirin, Ibuprofen, allergy tablets, nail clippers, tweezers, scissors, clear plasters, brush and comb, magnifying shaving mirror, whistles, penknives, passport and money cases, compass, head torches, earplugs, tin foil, cling film, Ziploc bags, rubbish bags, toilet rolls, travel washing powder, clothes lines, guidebooks, reading books, two Russian phrase books, binoculars, pens, string, strong cord, rubber bands, strong glue, black binliners, postcards, stickers, cigarette battery charger plus rechargeable batteries, Dictaphones, iPods and chargers.

Communications and navigation

Two of: Iridium phone, cellphone, phone chargers, Garmin GPS unit.

Video and photography equipment

Two of: on-bike camera, Panasonic NV-GS70 camcorder (plus allied car battery charger, stereo zoom microphone, filter kit, lens protector), digital stills camera (plus additional battery, charger and memory cards), 35mm stills camera. Tripod and mini-tripod. Mini DV tapes.

Bike spares on support vehicle

Eighteen Continental tyres (three sets for three bikes), replacement bulbs covering headlight main and dip beam, side lights, indicators and brake light, three sets of rear brake pads, pad retaining pins and anti-rattle clips, six sets of front brake pads, pad retaining pins and anti-rattle clips, spare front and rear ABS wheel sensors, eight front wheel spokes with mounting nipples and securing grub screws, eight rear wheel spokes with mounting nipples and securing grub screws, two sets of replacement front wheel bearings, two replacement saddles, low height option, three fuel octane coding relays (for poor fuel quality), three oil filters, six air filters, four replacement rocker cover gaskets, six spare spark plugs, two front brake levers, two clutch levers, three oil-pressure switches, three auxiliary power sockets.

Also on support vehicle

Full bike tool set, Charley's personal box, Ewan's personal box, extra clothes, extra helmets, extra motorbike boots, extra videotape, extra film, extra food.

Ending with a sense of hope

When Unicef invited us to see its work helping and protecting some of the world's most vulnerable children, neither of us had anticipated it would have such an impact. The three visits to Unicef projects in Mongolia, Ukraine and Kazakhstan stand out as some of the highlights of our journey.

We were able to catch a rare glimpse of the kind of bravery that some children need to survive, growing up alone, in poverty, at serious risk of exploitation and largely forgotten by the rest of the world. From the boys we met that sleep in the filthy manholes of Ulaanbaatar and the young people living with the fatal legacy of Chernobyl, to those uprooted and displaced by poverty in Almaty, their unfortunate stories were powerful and shocking. It is hard to believe that life can be so bleak at such a young age.

But what will remain in our memories is a sense of hope, because in each country we saw that something was being done to help. Unicef was taking action. Their staff – real heroes to the cause – work with a tireless passion and purpose to make a lasting, positive change for children. They have been an inspiration to us. Unicef is successfully giving children and young people all over the world opportunities and hope. Just like the ones we met. Unicef is protecting them from exploitation and is giving them the chances that we all take for granted.

As fathers, we know what a force for life children can be. They represent all of our futures. This trip has offered us the opportunity to help Unicef and to see first hand some of the life-changing work they're doing in the world.

We support Unicef; we hope you will do the same.

Charley Boorman and *Ewan McGregor*

unicef 🌐

UNICEF, the United Nations Children's Fund, is the world's largest organisation working specifically for children, protecting and promoting their rights. It works in 157 countries of the world to help every child reach their full potential through long term and emergency work on child health and nutrition, quality basic education for all boys and girls, and the protection of children from violence, exploitation and AIDS.

By working in partnership with others, from governments and teachers to youth groups and mothers, UNICEF is a driving force for people throughout the world working to ensure a better future for children.

UNICEF receives no funding from the UN, and relies entirely on voluntary donations to fund its work. UNICEF needs people like you to help protect children from exploitation and to build a world fit for children. You can make a difference. You can donate, or purchase UNICEF cards and gifts, or become a volunteer or campaigner.

If you are in the UK and would like to find out about giving, purchasing cards and gifts, volunteering or campaigning, please visit www.unicef.org.uk/longwayround

You can also donate by calling the 24-hour credit card hotline, quoting 'LWR' on: 08457 312 312, or by sending a cheque, payable to 'UNICEF' to:

UNICEF / 'LWR'
Freepost CL885
Billericay CM12 OBR
United Kingdom

If you are outside the UK and want to find out how you can get involved in your country or make a donation please visit www.supportunicef.org

Ewan and Charley also support the following charities:

Caring for a child who will die prematurely is one of the hardest things a family could face. The Children's Hospice Association Scotland (CHAS) is there to help the whole family. It runs Rachel House Children's Hospice in Kinross and the charity is now building its second hospice, Robin House, in Balloch. CHAS also provides a hospice at home service in the Scottish Highlands and Islands.
Our website is www.chas.org.uk

Children's Hospice Association Scotland
Sharing the Caring

Macmillan Cancer Relief provides the expert care and emotional support that makes a real difference to people living with cancer. We offer a range of innovative cancer services and are at the heart of improving cancer care throughout the UK.
Our website is www.macmillan.org.uk

In aid of

Picture credits

With thanks to:

Photographer	Page numbers
David Alexanian	25 (bottom left), 107, 125 (both), 134–5, 138 (both), 234–5, 240–1, 259
Charley Boorman	50 (left), 68–69, 72, 73, 90 (both), 104–5, 113, 132, 184 (top), 186–7, 210, 260–1
Julian Broad	Endpapers, 6–7, 10–11, 14, 15, 18–19, 28–29, 42–43, 60–61, 67, 80–81, 94–95, 96–97, 101, 116–7, 118–9, 124, 140–1, 144, 148–9, 163, 174–5, 190–1 (both), 192 (all), 194, 195 (all), 204–5, 226 (top left), 237 (bottom), 252–3, 284
Ewan McGregor	24 (top), 50 (right), 51, 54, 76, 85, 99, 102, 105 (top), 108, 108–9, 152, 156–7, 158, 162 (top), 167, 208–9, 215, 218–9 (top), 230, 254, 258 (top), 259 (top), 265 (top right)
Jim King	24 (bottom), 37 (bottom)
Russ Malkin	38, 39 (both), 40, 40–41, 92, 93, 103, 127, 129, 136–7, 142, 146–7 (all), 218–9 (bottom), 222, 231, 236 (bottom), 243, 244–5, 246, 248 (both), 249, 251, 258, 272 (both), 275, 276 (top), 277
Claudio von Planta	57, 121, 165, 168–9, 172–3, 178, 183, 198–9, 200, 203, 225 (both), 226, 229, 232–3, 236 (top left), 236 (second from top), 236 (top right), 237 (top left), 237 (top right), 237 (middle), 244, 245, 274
Jim Simak	2–3, 24 (bottom), 25 (both photos bottom right), 31 (both), 32–33, 35, 37 (top), 49 (both), 58–59, 71, 75, 89, 91, 110–1, 115, 122–3, 130, 143, 153, 154, 155, 160–1, 162 (bottom), 177, 179 (both), 180–1, 184 (bottom), 189, 197, 201, 212–3, 216–7, 228, 238–9, 253, 266, 267, 269, 287
Unicef	86–7
(Unknown)	25 (top), 48, 55, 56, 109, 112, 126, 222–3 (top), 223, 264 (all), 265 (top right and bottom six pictures)

Every effort has been made to credit the appropriate photographers in this book.
The publisher regrets any oversight and will be pleased to rectify any omission in future editions.

Acknowledgements

Very special thanks to:

Olivia, Doone, Kinvara and the whole Boorman and Cook clan
Eve, Clara, Esther and our family

Russ Malkin and David Alexanian, our partners.

Alexis Alexanian, Luke Boyle, Julian Broad, Totty Douglas, Ailsa Fereday,
John Ferriter, Manus Fraser, Julia Frater, Sergey Grabovets, Kash Javaid,
Lindy King, Robert Kirby, Asia Mackay, Jo Melling, Andrew Mer,
Rachel Newnham, Vasiliy Nisichenko, Ciara Parkes, Claudio von Planta,
Jake Roberts, James Simak, Lucy Trujillo, Robert Uhlig and Scott Waxman.

Tamsin Barrack, Antonia Hodgson, Caroline Hogg, Marie Hrynczak,
David Kent, Alison Lindsay, Nick Ross, Duncan Spilling, Diane Spivey and
David Young at Time Warner Book Group UK, and Janet James.

BMW Motorrad GB: Tony Jakeman, Pieter de Waal, Steve Bellars,
Howard Godolphin, Tony Jakeman

British Airways: Murray Lambell, Clare Sweeney

Mitsubishi: Gabi Whitfield

Sonic Communications: David Bryan, Darren Roper, Liam Thornton.

Unicef: Sarah Epstein, Alison Tilbe and Wendy Zych

TBR: Chris and Ivor